iron fists

branding the 20th-century totalitarian state

steven heller

introduction

Fascism is the aestheticizing of politics.
—Walter Benjamin

Starting in the twentieth century, totalitarian states began using the same graphic identity techniques as modern industries and corporations. Despots and businessmen alike strove to establish branding narratives, supported by visual images—logos and trademarks—that were used to trigger instantaneous recognition of their ideas and products. The goal was to ensure "brand loyalty," the ultimate objective of every branding strategy. "Twenty years before Madison Avenue embarked upon 'Motivational Research,' Hitler was systematically exploring and exploiting the secret fears and hopes, the cravings, anxieties and frustrations of the German masses," wrote Aldous Huxley in *Brave New World Revisited*, his 1958 critique of the modern methods of manipulating popular opinion.[1]

On the one hand, modern totalitarian states market themselves both to reinforce their power over a captive populace obliged to consume the dominant ideology and to extend the reach of that ideology to the hold-outs, the not yet captive, and the next generation. Corporate branding, on the other hand, is ostensibly a benign practice, intended to convince consumers to make informed choices. Still, it is never neutral. The aim of strategic branding is not merely to raise visibility in the marketplace by celebrating the intrinsic worth of an idea or product but also to infiltrate the subconscious in order to trigger conformist behavior (i.e., fealty to the brand).

The real objective of commercial branding campaigns is not to create "educated consumers," but rather to capture the loyalty of a targeted, and hopefully malleable, demographic. If this requires engaging in some ruse or creating a fallacy, then ruse and fallacy it is.

Comparing how corporations and dictatorial states are marketed may seem improbable: A popular brand of frozen food or laundry detergent is not forced down the consumer's throat with an iron fist; and even if these products monopolized the shelves, they would not have the same intimidating impact as Fascist or Communist diktats. Still, the design and marketing methods used to inculcate doctrine and guarantee consumption are fundamentally similar. And branding is not just smoke and mirrors; the results are often quantifiable because public awareness and brand loyalty can be measured by sales—or votes.

This book explores how four of the most destructive twentieth-century totalitarian regimes—Nazi Germany, Fascist Italy, Soviet Russia, and Communist China—proved to be extremely creative in their use of new branding strategies to sell their political messages. These regimes were selected for the diabolically effective ways in which their propaganda machinery created powerful visual narratives to seduce their respective populations. In each case, they developed unique visual schemes that triggered immediate recognition. The symbols and design objects devised as rallying points were so alluring on aesthetic as well as formalistic levels that they captured the attention of the world. Other dictatorships have used similar techniques, but they essentially copied the masters of the form, and rarely with the same visual impact. Francisco Franco in Spain, Juan Perón in Argentina, and Kim Il-sung in North Korea, for example, were not originators but merely imitators with their own national dialects. The Nazis, Fascists, Soviets, and Chinese Communists are thus the case studies by which modern totalitarian branding can best be analyzed.

The major component of any branding strategy is the logo—here, the swastika, *fascio*, hammer and sickle, and Chinese star—but other mnemonic elements are also useful. Branding campaigns often rely on characters, based on real or imagined people or things, to catapult the brand into the mass consciousness. Many corporations invest heavily in the creation of these "trade characters": the common (and often comic) metaphoric or anthropomorphic personifications seen on television commercials and in print advertisements, like Mr. Clean, Joe Camel, and Ronald McDonald. By imbuing products with fanciful—indeed likeable—human characteristics, the trade character puts a friendly face on an otherwise inanimate (or sometimes inhumane) product. The "Bib," or Michelin Man, one of the most famous international trade characters, has been hawking tires for over one hundred years, while today the Geico "Gecko" triggers such impromptu good will toward the auto insurance company that it has become a culture hero with its own blog.

These commercial examples are benign compared to the ways totalitarian regimes create mesmerizing auras around the stern visages of their leaders, but the principle is the same. What were the führer, Il Duce, Comrade Lenin, and Chairman Mao but a kind of ideological trade character? The concept of dictator as trade character may seem to trivialize, yet it is apt. All of the leaders discussed

in this book deliberately emphasized certain personal characteristics (Hitler's mustache, Mussolini's baldness, Lenin's goatee, Mao's Mona Lisa smile), with the aim of transforming their corporeal selves into icons. Then, in every possible public venue, they made themselves omnipresent, whether depicted in action or repose, meeting and greeting their subjects, or standing heroically tall above them. As ubiquitous as any commercial character, the leader's image on everything from monuments to postage stamps served the same purpose: as the instantly recognizable face of the regime.

Totalitarian states commonly issued strict laws protecting their national symbols, comparable to copyright and trademark protections held by commercial corporations. The Nazis, for example, who paid unrelenting attention to the minutest details, prohibited flagrant commercial use of Hitler's image, which was restricted to official party or state documents. Souvenir postcards and portraits could be sold commercially only through the firm of Hitler's official photographer, Heinrich Hoffmann—with the royalties going to Hitler himself. To make certain that the Hitler brand was untouchable, the head of the German Labor Front and custodian of Nazi party "identity," Robert Ley, decreed that nobody but Hitler could be called "führer" (leader). Conversely, Mussolini did allow sanctioned non governmental use of his portraits, which were found in certain retail advertisements (an interesting twist on product placement) to support the impression that he was a man of the people.

Effective branding is centered on a core narrative, and these totalitarian regimes offered two parallel stories, one rooted in hate, the other projecting a utopian future. Hitler's rant against the Jews was inextricably linked to the Nazi belief that German superiority would lead to world domination. Mussolini's screeds against the bourgeoisie were conflated with his imperial desires. Lenin exhorted workers of the world to break the shackles of despised capitalism to achieve the utopian freedoms of a classless society. And Mao's hatred for the "antirevolutionary" Communist establishment that threatened his hegemony was counterbalanced by his alleged commitment to building China's economic might. "The survival of democracy depends on the ability of large numbers of people to make realistic choices in the light of adequate information," wrote Huxley. "A dictatorship, on the other hand, maintains itself by censoring or distorting the facts, and by appealing, not to reason, not to enlightened self-interest, but to passion and prejudice, to the powerful 'hidden forces,' as Hitler called them, present in the unconscious depths of every human mind."[2] Each totalitarian brand story was designed both to enrage and to engage the populace.

The regimes discussed here—two Fascist and two Communist—were natural enemies, yet they shared a taste for monumentalism and heroic realism. What they didn't have in common was modernism. The Nazis dismissed modernism in favor of the antediluvian Aryan myths they resurrected as plotlines for their brand narrative. The Communist Chinese rejected all things old as representative of bourgeois decadence, yet without adopting modernism; Mao abjured creativity in favor of political pragmatism. The Italians and Soviets, on the other hand, began by embracing modernism as a sign of progress, and both profited from the initial enthusiasm generated by their regimes among the avant-garde. The Fascists leaned backward and forward, alternately adopting the trappings both of ancient Rome and of the Futurists; in the Soviet Union under Stalin, any vestige of progressive art was eventually annihilated in favor of Socialist Realism.

Branding a totalitarian state demands a sweeping vision that encompasses both the grand and the minute. In addition to mammoth monuments to Fascism and Communism, which were designed to dwarf the individual, even the smallest quotidian objects were stamped with the symbols and signs that made the regime seem omniscient and thus integral to the individual's daily life. The artifacts produced by and for the totalitarian state are therefore numerous and ubiquitous. Today history books, museums, libraries, and flea markets are replete with official icons—and souvenirs—of Nazi Germany, Fascist Italy, the Soviet Union, and the People's Republic of China. Showing the swastika is forbidden in Germany except for artistic, documentary, and educational purposes, but Nazi memorabilia can be readily found in flea markets and antique stores. The abundance of official "stuff" containing countless iterations of symbolic and representational graphics is not surprising, since the original goal was to flood the market with signs of allegiance.

The swastika, *fascio*, hammer and sickle, and Chinese star were complemented by scores of what in the branding field are called "ancillary" symbols designed to reinforce the "brand experience." In commercial terms, this means anything from stickers to clothes emblazoned with logos and trade characters. In political terms it means badges, armbands, posters, and other effluvia that are easy to mass produce. Porcelain workshops in China, for example, cranked out millions of souvenir figurines of Mao, similar to religious votives or commercial mascots. In Germany and Italy, hierarchical distinctions were emphasized by aesthetic devices both overt and subtle. Party uniforms included marks to distinguish between high and low ranks, as well as between average and elite divisions. (The Soviets and the Communist Chinese, on the other hand, reinforced the illusion of classlessness through their undifferentiated garb.) These elaborate uniforms, impressive badges, and other branded regalia were available in abundance, as were events to which to wear them, including spectacles that subsumed individuals into a branded mass. "Marching diverts men's thoughts," wrote Huxley. "Marching is the indispensable magic stroke performed in order to accustom the people to a mechanical, quasi-ritualistic activity until it becomes second nature."[3]

Rather than survey the official "high art" of each nation, this book concentrates on the popular art distributed en masse in the effort to capture the minds, if not the soul, of the people. "There are no masterpieces," Huxley said, "for masterpieces appeal only to a limited audience"[4] and the propagandist—the branding expert—has to reach as many people as possible. Even though some of the individual artifacts are remarkably well designed and crafted, the ideal was to attain what Huxley called "moderate excellence," which is appealing but never goes over anyone's head.

Explaining the visual language and branding strategies of these totalitarian regimes is essential to an understanding of how they developed, communicated, and perpetuated their core ideologies through word, picture, and design; how they seduced their followers and, curiously, their enemies as well. Much of this material is brilliant on what Huxley called a "supramundane level"; he qualified this by adding: "On the levels of politics and theology, beauty is perfectly compatible with nonsense and tyranny."[5] These totalitarian states used branding strategies for diabolical purposes, and they did so with undeniable effectiveness, which is what made them so dangerously beguiling.

the nazis

creating symbols

It is by manipulating 'hidden forces' that the advertising experts induce us to buy their wares—a toothpaste, a brand of cigarettes, a political candidate....Hitler induced the German masses to buy themselves a Führer, an insane philosophy, and the Second World War.
—Aldous Huxley, *Brave New World Revisited*, 1958

the leader as designer

Adolf Hitler wanted to become a serious artist; he applied twice to the prestigious Vienna Akademie der Bildenden Künste (Academy of Fine Arts), but was rejected both times. He frequently said that art, not politics, was his true calling. Joseph Goebbels, the infamous Nazi minister of propaganda, reinforced the image by claiming that Hitler was an artist who went into politics to relieve the suffering German nation, and he promised that after winning the war Hitler would focus exclusively on matters of art. Hitler viewed art as little more than the replication of nature, and his early watercolors of still lifes, landscapes, and buildings evidence his unyielding emphasis on academic craft. But he had a perverse vision, too, for in some of his studies from 1913–14 he conceived an elaborate dystopia where the overall imagery—including uniforms, flags, and symbols— constituted a kind of sociopolitical art project. In this Hitlerian worldview, culture and politics were intricately woven into a grand opera in which aesthetics integral to his extremist ideology played a leading role in an absurdist fantasy that could not possibly occur in real life. Or could it? When the Nazis seized power in 1933, Hitler's entire conceptualization was immediately put into practice.

It could be argued that this self-proclaimed artist conceived his horrific plans as a massive sociopolitical *Gesamtkunstwerk* (total work of art) built on the notions of racial purification, nationalist regeneration, and world domination. These were integrated in an overall graphic scheme, much of which Hitler either designed himself or had a hand in designing. It does raise the question of why the audacious visual identity of Nazi Germany was so extraordinarily effective, and how it ultimately became a textbook example—indeed, a perverse paradigm—of corporate branding.

Hitler's artistic aspirations were instrumental in helping him achieve his heinous political goals. He acutely understood the value of art and design in rallying the masses and manufacturing consent. Once the apparatus that combined propaganda and coercion was finely tuned, the masses succumbed to Hitler's will—and to his aesthetic precepts as well. Thus, what might be called the "art dictatorial state" was born.

Two events were instrumental in directing Hitler's attention to the political power of graphic design. The more important of these was the German defeat in World War I, which in his view demonstrated the fact that Allied propaganda was overwhelmingly superior to the meager attempts of Kaiser Wilhelm II. While British and American propagandists successfully defamed the German "Hun" through a barrage of posters and other visual media, portraying the German monarchy and Junker military as beasts responsible for untold atrocities, the kaiser's counterattack was tepid at best. "The Germans were sent into this mighty battle with not so much as a single slogan," wrote the

1. **Nazi logo**
From mystical origins to political logo, the swastika was coopted by the Nazis and remains indelibly tied to the regime. Date unknown

2. **Nazi symbol**
Adolf Hitler's visage became the emblem of the Nazi state. This portrait by Hitler's personal photographer, Heinrich Hoffmann, appeared on the cover of the Nazi newspaper *Illustrierter Beobachter* (Illustrated observer) for a special issue on the führer. 1936

Background:
Swastikas hanging in the streets of Munich. c. 1935

Previous spread:
Young girls in Saarbrücken celebrate Hitler's birthday. 20 April 1935

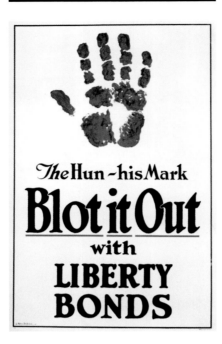

3. *In Deo Gratia*
(Thank be to God)
German World War I
poster by Fritz Boehle.
1915

4. *Blot It Out
with Liberty Bonds*
American World
War I poster,
designed by J. Allen
St. John, defaming
the German "Hun."
1917

5. *Das politische Plakat*
(The political poster)
Erwin Schockel's
analysis of the
psychological impact
of political posters
became a textbook
for Nazi poster design.
The inscription at the
bottom reads "Property
of the NSDAP."
1939

6. Swastikas on parade
Brownshirts and
Freikorps parade with
assorted early versions
of the Nazi flag.
1924

Nazi propaganda expert and Goebbels's deputy Eugen Hadamovsky.[1] Hitler took the power of the political poster very seriously, and after the Nazis came to power in 1933, they commissioned extensive research on the psychological effects of posters that resulted in Erwin Schockel's book *Das politische Plakat* (The political poster).[2] The book assessed the impact of English, American, French, and German political poster design during World War I. It was destined to be used as a textbook by German propagandists.

The second significant underpinning of Hitler's visual mission was his profound envy of the Bolshevik red flag and hammer-and-sickle emblems, which hung from apartment windows and were brandished by Communists during the street skirmishes between right and left factions that were so common in German cities after World War I. "More than once in my youth the psychological importance of such a symbol had become clearly evident to me," Hitler explained in his 1925 prison memoir *Mein Kampf* (My struggle). "In Berlin, after the war, I was present at a demonstration of Marxists in front of the Royal Palace and in the Lustgarten. A sea of red flags, red armlets and red flowers was in itself sufficient to give that huge assembly of about 120,000 persons an outward

appearance of strength. I was now able to feel and understand how easily the man in the street succumbs to the hypnotic magic of such a grandiose piece of theatrical presentation."[3]

Germany's defeat in World War I and the establishment of a fractious Weimar Republic ushered in a fragile economy and wounded cultural identity. As a result of violent tensions between right- and left-wing social and political factions, Germany was completely polarized. One of the things the Nazis purported to be offering the German population was the dream of social unification—glorious Teutonic cohesion—complete with a grandiose national history and a common mission to "purify" the Aryan race, all symbolized by coordinated graphic signifiers that served as visual reinforcement of the "common heritage" of all Germanic peoples.

Hitler was a great admirer of Peter Behrens, the father of the concept of modern corporate identity. In 1907 Behrens, a graphic and product designer and the artistic and design consultant for the Allgemeine Elektrizitäts-Gesellschaft (AEG), Germany's largest supplier of electricity, designed the first integrated corporate identity system. His striking honeycombed logotype with the initials

AEG was one of many components applied to the company's unprecedented overall branding campaign, which included advertising, packaging, product design, and architecture. This uniform system had a huge influence on scores of other German designers, and on Hitler. (In 1936 Hitler appointed Behrens to head the architecture section of the Prussian Academy of Art in Berlin.) Behrens did not invent the use of initials as a branding scheme (General Electric used GE as a logo prior to this), but it became the model for the Nazis, who reduced all party and government departments to initials and acronyms, and was eventually widely adopted by businesses.

Hitler joined the nascent right-wing Deutsche Arbeiterpartei (German Workers' Party) in 1919 as its public relations officer. After taking over the party in 1920 (and renaming it Nationalsozialistische Deutsche Arbeiterpartei—National Socialist German Workers' Party; NSDAP, or Nazi), he insisted that visual identity and graphic design be given the highest priority. "Up till then the movement had possessed no party badge and no party flag," he wrote in *Mein Kampf*. "The lack of these tokens was not only a disadvantage at that time but would prove intolerable in the future. The disadvantages were chiefly that members of the party possessed no outward [sign]

7. *Ein Kampf um Deutschland* (A battle for Germany)
This hand-colored photomontage pamphlet cover, designed by Tibor, illustrates the conflict between the Nazis and their Communist adversaries. 1933

of membership which linked them together, and it was absolutely unthinkable that for the future they should remain without some token which would be a symbol of the movement and could be set against that of the [Communist] International."[4] He immediately called for a well-defined identity system to distinguish his party and its members from the opposition— as well as from the past. In addition to the party's emblem and membership badge, Hitler designed its stationery, rubber stamps (the German bureaucrats couldn't function without their rubber stamps), and the masthead of the party newspaper. In his otherwise plodding rant of a book, *Mein Kampf*, he convincingly sets down rationales for a systematic design program based entirely on memorable signs and symbols:

"All those who busy themselves with the tastes of the public will recognize and appreciate the great importance of these apparently petty matters. In hundreds of thousands of cases a really striking emblem may be the first cause of awakening interest in a movement," he wrote.[5] "Through his aesthetic sensibility Hitler…had an instinctive understanding of the emotive power of symbols…and applied this in designing the party's iconography," writes Frederic Spotts in *Hitler and the Power of Aesthetics*. "None of the basic ideas originated with him. His genius lay in knowing which symbols to choose and how to present them in an arresting way."[6]

Hitler, who treasured the Iron Cross he had won during World War I (it was the only decoration he wore on his party uniform), understood that members were more apt to follow if they shared in the trappings of the party. Acknowledging that he had a personal attachment to the national colors under which he had fought as a soldier, he nonetheless deliberately dismissed any suggestions that proposed using the old state colors, to make a clear break with the past and avoid any analogy "with those decrepit parties whose sole political objective is the restoration of past conditions."[7] In addition, he held that only certain colors were capable of attracting and focusing public attention, especially during a period of revolution. Using a semiotician's logic, he rejected pure white (too insignificant) or black (strong, but incapable of attracting attention alone), and any "weak" color combinations. He had many visual ideas of his own, but preferred not to disclose them in order to leave all options open without losing face. "I, as leader, was unwilling to make public my own design, as it was possible that someone else could come forward with a design just as good, if not better, than my own."[8]

After various iterations, Hitler decided upon a final form—a red flag emblazoned with a white disk and a black swastika in its middle. He explained that the red expressed the social thought underlying the movement; white, the national thought; and the swastika signified the struggle for the victory of "Aryan mankind and at the same time the triumph of the ideal of creative work which is in itself and always will be anti-Semitic."[9] Hitler boasted that it was the perfect evocation of a revolutionary movement: "new and young."[10] The new flag appeared for the first time in the summer of 1921. Since no one had seen the flag before its unfurling, "its effect at that time was something akin to that of a blazing torch," he crowed. "We ourselves experienced almost a boyish delight when one of the ladies of the party who had been entrusted with the making of the flag finally handed it over to us. And a few months later those of us in Munich were in possession of six of these flags."[11]

the swastika

Although the swastika had been a sign of German nationalism before Hitler took an interest in it, it also had other meanings that were not at all part of the Nazi liturgy. To understand the magnitude of the symbol's effect and its perverse adoption, it is important to review its legacy. "Perhaps der Führer is unaware that the cross of which the swastika is a variation was used in charms and amulets by Jews long before the birth of Aryanism," exclaimed a letter writer to the *New York Times* on 6 May 1938.[12] Hitler was, in fact, well aware of the symbol's origins but did his utmost to rewrite its history to fit the Nazi myth.

The swastika is one of humankind's oldest symbols. It represents prosperity and good fortune, and numerous meanings have been ascribed to it. It indicates the course of the sun revolving from left to right; it symbolizes light, lightning, rain, and water. It has been recognized as representing the generative principle of mankind, making it the symbol of the female. It is believed to be a Jain icon representing animal, human, and celestial life. It is also a sign of Brahma, Vishnu, and Siva, and appears carved in the footprints of Buddha in the mountains of India. It is similar to the ancient Hebrew letter tau, the sign of life. Swastika decorations were found during the archaeological excavation of Troy; they were also discovered painted or etched into Etruscan pottery, Cyprian vases, and Corinthian coins. Known in England and Scotland as the *fylfot* (many feet), the swastika was the embodiment of auspicious beginnings. It was frequently found on Native American blankets and beadwork.

The swastika was adopted by many secret societies, including the Masonic order and the Theosophist movement. The writer Rudyard Kipling, who led anti-German propaganda efforts in England during World War I, used it as a personal logo, emblazoned on the covers of his books (he relinquished this habit in 1933, after the Nazis took

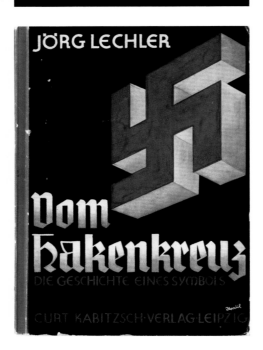

8. *5000 Jahre Hakenkreuz, Heilszeichen der Germanen* (5,000 years of the swastika, symbol of the Germans) Illustrated Nazi history of the swastika, designed for schoolchildren. 1935

9. *Vom Hakenkreuz, die Geschichte eines Symbols* (The swastika, history of a symbol) Heavily illustrated Nazi history of the swastika by Jörg Lechler. 1934

10. *Das Program der N.S.D.A.P. und seine weltanschaulichen Grundgedanken* (The program of the NSDAP and the worldview on which it is based) Gottfried Feder was the Nazi party's early economic theoretician. His anticapitalist views were exposed in this 1927 treatise. The cover for the 1931 edition was unusually typeset entirely in sans serif. 1931

power). During World War I, the American Forty-fifth Infantry Division adopted as its shoulder patch a yellow swastika on a red field, the four "legs" of the swastika representing the four states of the Forty-fifth Division: Oklahoma, Arizona, Colorado, and New Mexico. The insignia was changed to a thunderbird in 1939. In the 1930s the swastika was used on the national flags of Estonia, Latvia, and Finland (where it was known as the *hakaristi*, the cross of freedom, and used on warplanes that were not allied to the Nazis).

There could not have been an organization or institution more benign than the Swastika Clubs, representing various social or professional groups, which were formed throughout the United States in the 1910s and 1920s. Of these, the Girls' Club offered a nationally distributed monthly magazine called *Swastika*.[13] Each issue bore a cover illustration that cleverly integrated the swastika motif into an illustrative vignette. The club's official award was a diamond-studded swastika pin. The Boy Scouts established their own "Order of the White Swastika," which tested a scout's physical endurance. (Not until 1940 did Boy and Girl Scout leaders abandon the swastika as the symbol of distinguished service.)

The swastika was often used for commercial purposes. In 1910 the Excelsior Shoe Company, manufacturers of the original Boy Scout shoe, used the swastika as a logo and issued a swastika-emblazoned token as an advertising premium. It was adopted by German manufacturers and industries and incorporated onto machines, posters, advertisements, and poster-stamps—until in 1933 the Nazis officially prohibited the use of the swastika as a commercial mark.

The meaning was forever changed when the Nazis co-opted it. In taking the swastika as the symbol for his extremist nationalist party, Hitler followed a number of mystic and *völkisch* (folkish—signifying the philosophical return to a racially pure, fundamentalist ideal of ancient German culture) nationalist orders and lodges that had emerged throughout Germany and Austria after the turn of the century. These societies, which wed racialism and Gnostic mysticism, adopted the swastika as a symbol of Aryan transcendence. German occultists saw the swastika as the sacred sign of an ancient Indo-European elite—an Aryan race—that according to myth had once ruled Teutonic Europe and was destined to regain power within Germany and eventually over the world.

One of the most important figures of Germanic
revivalism was Guido von List, who at the turn of the
twentieth century created a neopagan occultist society,
the Armanenschaft (Armanen brotherhood), based
on the esoteric doctrines of the gnosis and the magical
power of runes. In his 1908 treatise *Das Geheimnis
der Runen* (The secret of the runes), List held the
swastika—which represented the sun—to be one
of the Armanen's holiest symbols. List also advocated
a Gothic revival in Germany. He contended that Gothic
architecture contained ancient secrets with roots
in Armanenism and, in his publications, encouraged
the use of spiky Fraktur type, which he contended
evoked the glorified past.

Influenced by List, Jörg Lanz von Liebenfels,
a self-proclaimed gnostic who founded the medievalist
New Templars in 1907, developed an ideology based
on Aryanism and inferior races. He published *Ostara:
Briefbücherei der Blonden und Mannesrechtler* (Ostara:
Newsletter of the fair-haired fighters for the rights
of men),[14] a nationalist and anti-Semitic periodical,
which also used the swastika as its emblem. Hitler was
a frequent reader of *Ostara*, and the roots of Heinrich
Himmler's Lebensborn maternity organization
can probably be traced back to the magazine, which
was replete with notions of race purification through
farmed pregnancies and ethnic cleansing. Yet after
the Nazis came to power, Lanz's writing was banned,
perhaps as a way for Hitler to disavow the fact that
he had been influenced by anyone.

The Thule Society is the *völkisch* group most
closely linked to the Nazi party. In 1918 Rudolf von
Sebottendorff, grand master of the Bavarian chapter
of the Germanenorden Walvater (a schismatic division
of the occult group the Germanenorden, or Teutonic
Order) renamed the organization the Thule Society,
which in 1919 established the German Workers'
Party (the political party that Hitler joined, took over,
and transformed into the Nazi party). Sebottendorff's
influence on the visual marks of the Thule Society

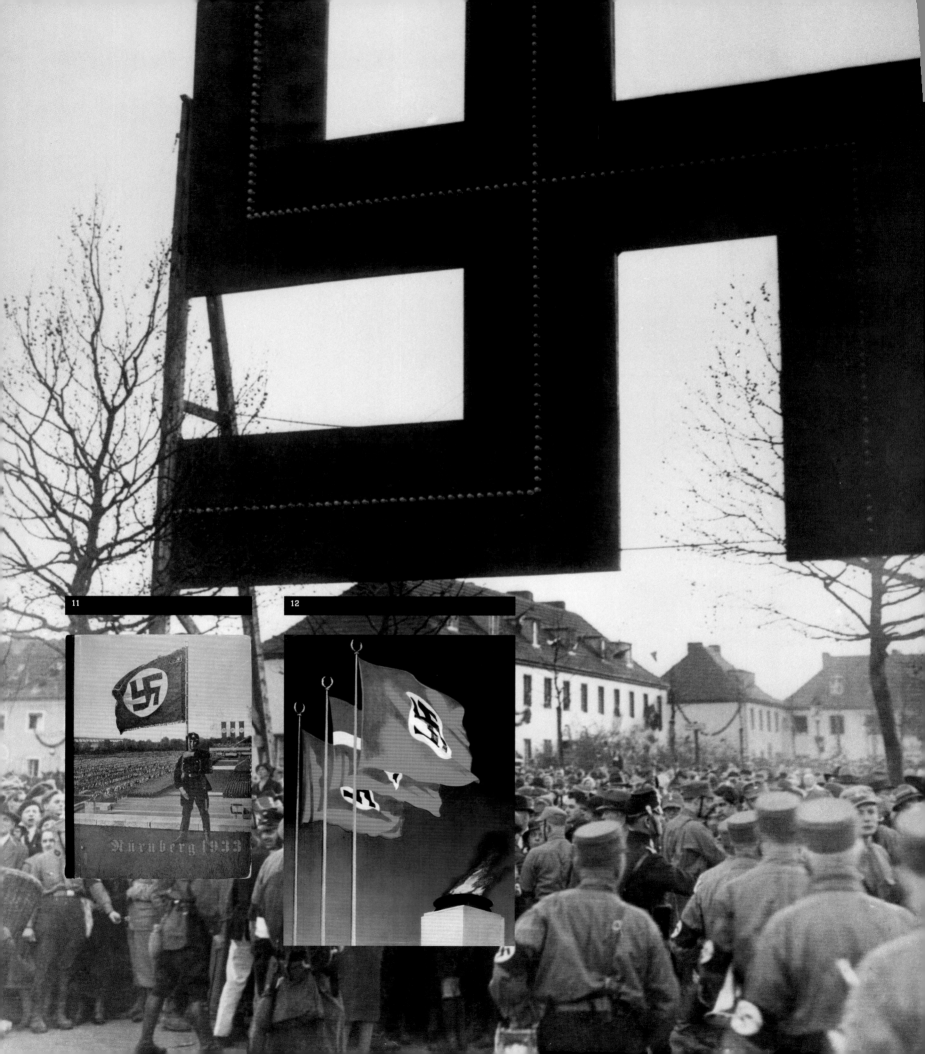

presage those later used by the Nazi party. He selected as the society's emblem a long dagger superimposed against a curved swastika. He introduced an additional symbol into the language of *völkisch* occultism: the Ar-rune, which signifies Aryan primal fire, the sun, and the eagle. "The eagle," he announced, "is the symbol of the Aryans. In order to depict the eagle's capacity for self-immolation by fire, it is colored red. From today on our symbol is the red eagle, which warns us that we must die in order to live." Sebottendorff appears to have inspired Nazi liturgy in yet another way: he instituted the *Sieg Heil* (hail victory), which later became the primary Nazi salute, as his order's greeting.

During World War I the Wandervogel (Migratory Birds), a German youth movement many of whose members became army officers, adopted the swastika as a nationalist symbol. After Germany's defeat in 1918, numerous veterans banded in paramilitary organizations known as Freikorps (Free Corps) or Stalhelm (Steel Helmet) to fight against those they held responsible for the debacle—Communists, republicans, and Jews. These veterans were frequently employed by the Weimar government to carry out illicit acts of violence against Communists. It was the infamous Erhardt Brigade, whose members wore swastikas on their steel helmets, that crushed the local coup attempted by Bolsheviks in Munich in 1919 to oust the fledgling Weimar Republic.

It is easy to follow the trajectory of the swastika's use by occult groups, which ultimately resulted in its appropriation by the Nazis. Yet the manner of its adoption was deliberately obscured by Hitler, who sought to detach the swastika from its occult history to ensure its reincarnation as a political symbol. Like any savvy corporate leader, Hitler took ownership of the *Hakenkreuz*, as the swastika is called in German, as his exclusive invention. In his early role as public-relations officer for the German Workers' Party, he had designed maquettes using varying swastika motifs

for the party's posters and emblems. During that time Hitler was undoubtedly influenced by other swastika designs, but he ultimately denied the influence of others. For example, Dr. Friedrich Krohn, another member of the Nazi party known for his scholarship in *völkisch* symbology, wrote a report in 1919 titled "Is the Swastika Suitable as the Symbol of the National Socialist Party?" in which he attempted to prove that the symbol was Germanic and Aryan.[15] In this report Krohn proposed a curved sun-wheel version of the swastika and the color combination of red, black, and white, as well as the clockwise version of the symbol. Hitler ultimately chose a rectilinear design but favored the clockwise version. However, he justified his preference by saying that he had seen a similar swastika on the coat of arms of Lambach Abbey, which he had visited in Austria.[16]

Similarly, Hitler failed to credit Wilhelm Deffke, whose Wilhelmwerk was a leading logo and trademark design studio, for having refined and stylized a version of the swastika very similar to the Nazi swastika prior to 1920. In the 1960s Deffke's former assistant wrote in a letter to the designer Paul Rand: "[Deffke] came across a representation of the ancient Germanic sun wheel on which he worked to redefine and stylize its shape. Later on this symbol appeared in a brochure which he had published; [the Nazis] chose it as their symbol but reversed it.... Needless to say, this was done without any thought of copyright or compensation."[17] In *Mein Kampf* Hitler contends: "I myself…after innumerable attempts, had laid down a final form.... After long trials I also found a definite proportion between the size of the flag and the size of the white disk, as well as the shape and thickness of the swastika."[18]

In March 1933, on the eve of the election that would sweep the Nazis to power, the party published a flyer with the following words of advice: "It must be the duty of each fellow citizen who professes his allegiance to our Leader to demonstrate his loyalty

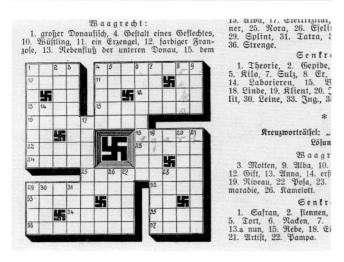

by adorning his dwelling on election day with the symbol of the New Germany, the swastika flag."[19] Shortly thereafter, on 19 May 1933, Joseph Goebbels decreed the *Verordnung über die Einführung des Gesetzes zum Schutze der nationalen Symbole* (law for the protection of national symbols), which prevented the unauthorized commercial use of the swastika. That same year the Nazi government declared that "the old black, white, and red colors of the imperial regime shall fly side by side with the Nazi swastika" on all public buildings in Germany.[20] Hitler described this in a speech as signifying "the puissant rebirth of the German nation."[21] In 1934 the *New York Times* optimistically wrote: "In accepting the imperial flag and the Nazi hooked-cross banner, President von Hindenburg accepts the political triumph of the parties of which they are the symbol, but his oath of allegiance to the Republic still stands inviolate."[22] But by 1935 Nazi power was absolute in Germany, Hitler wielded dictatorial control, and swastikas flew on all German properties, both at home and abroad. On 15 September 1935, the Nuremberg law making the swastika Germany's only national flag was enacted.

ARTICLE I: The Reich's colors are black, white and red.
ARTICLE II: The Reich and National flag is the swastika flag. It is also the merchant flag.[23]

On the same day, the first session of the Reichstag was convened in Nuremberg, rather than Berlin, during which the infamous "Jewish Laws" were put into effect, depriving Jews of German citizenship—which included prohibiting them from flying the national flag. Interior Minister Wilhelm Frick decreed: "The display of the national flags, especially the swastika flag, by Jews must cease."[24]

In only a few short years the swastika was transformed from an occult talisman to the inviolable symbol of Nazi Germany. Given the swastika's significance, after the Nazis' defeat and under the Allied strategy called "denazification," the prohibition of the symbol, and of other trappings of the Nazi brand, was absolute. To this day, the German criminal code permits the use of the swastika exclusively for artistic, scientific, research, or educational purposes. All other uses are unconstitutional.

hitler as icon, trademark, and mascot
Hitler's image was designed to become the face of the Nazi state. Referring to Hitler in his 1933 book *Propaganda und nationale Macht* (Propaganda and national power), Eugen Hadamovsky wrote: "No passion, no idea can find its final and strongest expression without the great symbol."[25] Rudolf Hess, Hitler's loyal factotum, put it this way: "One man remains always excluded from all criticism—the

13. Swastika crossword
Crossword puzzle in the Nazi newspaper *Völkischer Beobachter* (People's observer). 1937

14. Airborne swastika
Planes in swastika formation at the eleventh Nuremberg rally. 6 September 1937

15. Germany awake!
The *Deutschland Erwache* (Germany awake) standards, used by regional Nazi party chapters, were designed by Hitler based on a Roman model. Each standard features a German eagle holding a swastika within a laurel wreath, with the name of the chapter underneath. Date unknown

Führer. That is due to the fact that every one feels and knows: He was always right and will always be right."[26]

Hitler's identity was carefully crafted and skillfully stage-managed to represent both the omnipotent leader and the protector of the nation. He was at once the proverbial Big Brother and the "savior of the German race." After the death in 1934 of President Paul von Hindenburg (who, after the March 1933 election, had been compelled to appoint Hitler the Chancellor of Germany), Hitler dispensed with the title of president, suggesting that this honorific should always be associated with his predecessor. In doing so, Hitler discarded all semblance of the former republic. "I shall be addressed officially and privately only as 'der Führer' and Reich Chancellor. This regulation shall apply to all future time."[27] And Robert Ley, head of the German Labor Front and custodian of Nazi party "identity," decreed that nobody but Hitler could be called führer, even "in connection with another word."[28]

Hitler's visage became as ubiquitous as the swastika, but whether his portrait seemed official or candid, its appearance was never left to chance. Any pose that might deflate the myth was strictly avoided (for instance, he never allowed himself to be photographed with his glasses on, although images made public only after his demise show that he wore them). He was never shy before the camera, but his first real photographic "stylizing" opportunity occurred on the morning of 20 December 1924, following his release from the Landsberg prison, where he had served eight months of a five-year sentence for treason (the result of his failed attempt to overthrow the Weimar government). Hitler did not allow his personal photographer, Heinrich Hoffmann, to photograph him as he left the jail; Hoffmann was ordered instead to drive him to the imposing town-wall gate, where he shot Hitler wearing a belted trench coat, standing next to an impressive new motorcar. Hitler had adamantly refused to be seen emerging from such

16–17. Hitler
gesticulating
Hitler spent time
rehearsing his speeches
in front of Heinrich
Hoffmann's camera.
c. 1925

18. *Adolf Hitler der
deutsche Arbeiter
und Frontsoldat* (Adolf
Hitler, the German
worker and soldier)
This election
campaign brochure
features a portrait
by Hitler's designated
photographer,
Heinrich Hoffmann.
1932

19. Hitler souvenir
Commemorative
pamphlet for a sporting
event illustrated
by Nazi poster artist
Ludwig Hohlwein.
1936

20. Hitler postcard
Hoffmann photographed
Hitler in different
attire and situations,
and sold postcards of
these portraits.
c. 1930

21. Hitler bust
Effigies of the führer,
like this bust by
Arno Breker, were
displayed in all
government offices.
1939

Background:
Hitler's appearances
were carefully stage-
managed by his
close adviser and later
minister of propaganda
Joseph Goebbels
(at far right).
c. 1922

an inauspicious building as the prison, understanding
that to achieve the most dramatic return—and photo
opportunity—context was everything. The heroic
pose he chose was ultimately more newsworthy than
one showing his initial whiff of freedom; Hoffmann
submitted this photograph to various newspapers,
which gave it very prominent display. The photographer later recalled, "When I received my copies
I could not help laughing," knowing how this "first
small dishonesty by propaganda" had so successfully
manipulated the press.[29]

Hitler met Hoffmann early, even before he transformed the German Workers' Party into the NSDAP,
and Hoffmann soon became his official photographer
and confidant.[30] His publishing house, Heinrich
Hoffmann Verlag, was not owned by the NSDAP but
tethered to it. It produced catalogs featuring countless
Nazi images, including postcards, wall hangings,
portfolios, card decks, and even large and small

bronze busts of the führer as well as loose-leaf folios
of Hitler's watercolor paintings. There were also images
of prominent Nazis and Nazi party events. Hoffmann
made considerable profits from selling these images,
and devised a merchandising model that also made the
führer extremely wealthy: Hitler earned royalties for
the use of his image on everything from posters to
postage stamps.

Joseph Goebbels was instrumental in creating
a multilayered myth of the infallible führer. He coined
the slogan "Hitler over Germany," suggesting that
the "modern" leader was capable of unlimited
availability to the German people. This was achieved
by air travel: Although Hitler was not fond of flying,
he understood the benefits of being seen in three
cities in a single day. The illusion of proximity to the
people was further emphasized by the fabrication of
a sympathetic Hitler. Images of the führer patting
dogs, pinching the cheeks of young boys, and accepting

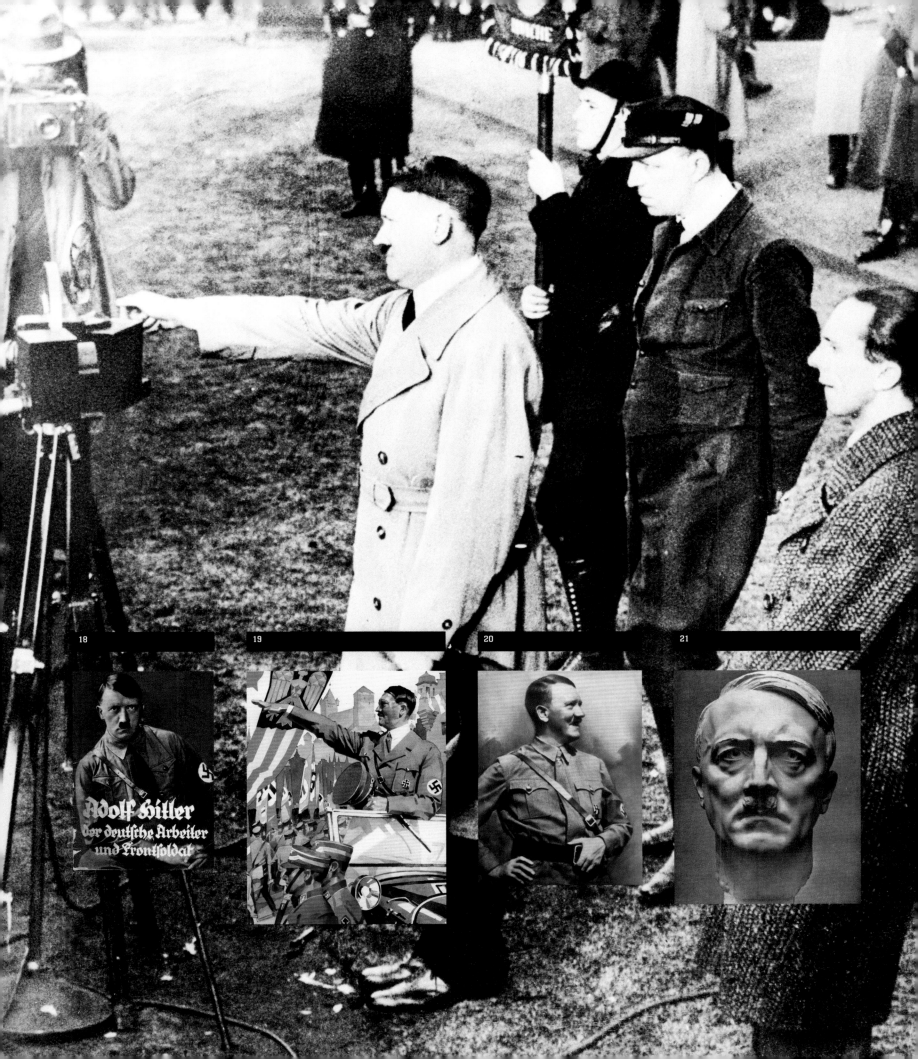

18 19 20 21

22. Release from Landsberg prison
After serving the minimum sentence for his attempted Munich Putsch, Hitler posed for a photograph by Heinrich Hoffmann designed to make him look like a hero, not a released prisoner. 1924

23. Hitler in pictures
Hoffmann made a fortune selling Hitler photos, postcards, and other memorabilia presented in this catalog. 1938

24–26. Hitler stamps
Hoffmann helped negotiate a deal with the German postmaster to pay Hitler a royalty for every stamp bearing his image. Hoffmann also received a percentage for the use of his photographs. 1934–40

27. Hitler postcard
The führer was often portrayed with young children to give his image a softer side. Postcard painted after a Hoffman photograph. c. 1938

flowers from young maidens were widely propagated. "The whole nation loves him, feels safe with him at the helm," the images said. The goal of the endless array of Nazi photographs, paintings, posters, and postage stamps was to ensure that followers maintained intimate identification with their leader—"Our Hitler," as some posters stated.

In the early years after the 1923 Munich Putsch, Hitler was barred from broadcasting, his newspapers suppressed and leaflets confiscated, so he took to the streets and stage as much as possible, where he honed his dexterity as a public speaker. His effectiveness as orator was not achieved through words alone, which were deliberately repetitive and usually platitudinous, but through his hypnotic rapport with the audience—the image he projected, the look he assumed. For every speech his opening movements were choreographed, so that every gesture seemed disarmingly hesitant, his body stiff. His voice was muted, as though speaking was uncomfortable for him. Then, after a few minutes, he grew more confident, more relaxed, more impassioned, and his voice became louder and clearer. Soon he began waving his fists, pounding on invisible nails as his voice reached a fevered pitch. This crescendo came abruptly, but his audience was so mesmerized by the flow of words that it didn't matter. Hitler also purposefully scheduled such events late at night, when the audience's suggestibility was high and resistance was low.

imperial symbols

While Hitler and the swastika were the principal visual assets of the Nazi identity, various other symbols reinforced the brand. The Grosse Deutschland eagle, borrowed from the classic imperial eagle dating back to the Roman Empire, was the most common Nazi symbol aside from the swastika. In its heroic stance, the eagle symbolized domination over the

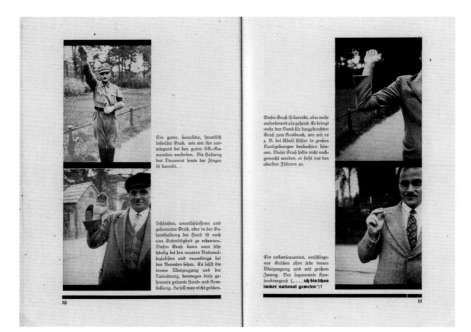

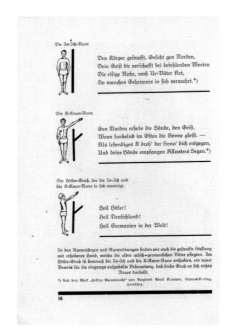

weak Weimar Republic and, in 1933, became the *Hoheitsabzeichen* (national emblem) of the Third Reich and appeared on various government flags. As the official symbol of Germany's imperial ambitions, it was designed in three basic iterations: as official party symbol with wings outstretched, its talons holding a wreath with swastika; as one with wings open but draped; and as if caught in the act of flying. Often the eagle was monumentalized, and not only as an ideological complement to the swastika, but alone. Eagles were designed in hundreds of iterations, both realistic and abstract, and used on all manner of paraphernalia, from military medallions and signs to police badges to railroad insignia, as well as travel advertisements and posters.

Hitler also borrowed the Roman salute from Mussolini (who had instituted it in Italy shortly after assuming power in 1922) as an ideological alternative to the bourgeois handshake. Hitler insisted, however, that it derived not from Rome but from a medieval German practice. In Germany the raised outstretched arm was dubbed the "German salute," and along with the greeting *Heil Hitler* (hail to Hitler), which replaced the conventional *guten Tag* (good day), symbolized fealty to the führer. The salute was used by all party members prior to 1933; after the takeover of power, all civil servants were ordered to use it as the official greeting. Reich Minister of the Interior Wilhelm Frick urged that the salute have nationwide application, and in July 1933 decreed "a task of popular enlightenment to introduce the German salute among all sections of the German people as the expression of national solidarity."[31] It was further decreed that this so-called salute of the free man not be used by inmates of penal institutions—nor, of course, by Jews. The appropriation of such a common, everyday greeting was the key to micromanaging public opinion and thoroughly inculcating the Nazi creed in the entire population.

30

31

32

33

34

ABC
des
Nationalsozialismus

Reichstag für Freiheit und Frieden
Wahlkreis

Nationalsozialistische Deutsche Arbeiterpartei
Adolf Hitler

Heß   Frick   Göring   Goebbels

propagating the brand

gleichschaltung

The Nazi machination that so successfully led to total control was their policy of *Gleichschaltung* (best translated as "synchronization"), the deliberate and systematic infiltration of Nazism into every aspect of German society. Everything from businesses to culture was to adhere to Nazi laws, mores, and aesthetics. The nation's art and design—including graphic design and advertising, typefaces, and illustration—came under the strict control of National Socialism. What made *Gleichschaltung* possible in the design sphere was the fact that a Nazi style was well established before Hitler took control of the state. The organizational handbook *ABC des Nationalsozialismus* (ABC of National Socialism) was published in 1933; it established overall rules for party leaders, including graphic standards. But more important, as Hitler proclaimed in *Mein Kampf*, the party's key graphic component, the swastika, already had pervasive visibility. Once the Nazis were in control of district government bureaus and state ministries, a national propaganda apparatus was easily put in place.

Upon the seizure of power by the Nazis, Joseph Goebbels, a dramatist, novelist, and journalist who became an avid follower of Hitler when he joined the party in 1924, became head of the National Ministry for Public Enlightenment and Propaganda (most often referred to in German simply as *Propagandaministerium*, or its contraction, *Promi*). The ministry dealt with "active propaganda," which included everything from political agitation to meetings to architectural design and pageants. It was organized in divisions that covered every imaginable aspect of social, communications, and cultural affairs and controlled everything from nationwide legislation to counterpropaganda. It also produced its own newspaper, *Unser Wille und Weg: Monatsblätter der Reichspropagandaleitung* (Our will and way: Monthly letters of propaganda management), which reported on methods of coercive communication. The Promi's central headquarters dictated to provincial offices that were administered through cells. As early as 1933 Goebbels also established the Reichskulturkammer (Reich Chamber of Culture), which exercised airtight control over every cultural mechanism. As president of the Chamber of Culture, Goebbels controlled the press, radio, film, literature, fine arts, theater, and music.

Together, the Promi and the Chamber of Culture ensured the integration of Nazi doctrines into the everyday life of the German people. Admittedly, Goebbels did not hold a monopoly on the branding of the Nazi state, and he fought bitter battles with many other officials for total authority. But regardless of who was personally in charge, Nazi institutions were absolutely in control.

To achieve Hitler's design, it was imperative that there be no opposition or overt criticism whatsoever.

33. *ABC des Nationalsozialismus* (ABC of National Socialism)
This handbook outlines in simple terms the early Nazi movement, its origins and goals, including portraits of its members, starting with Adolf Hitler. 1933

34. Reichstag ballot
Just one year after Hitler took power, the Nazi party appeared alone on the ballot to elect the leaders of the Reichstag. Votes were to be cast with a cross in the right-hand box. Ballots left blank were considered void. 1934

Background:
Members of the Reichstag salute Chancellor Hitler. 2 March 1938

Prior to 1933, Germany was awash with posters, flags, emblems, and uniforms representing the many opposing political factions. But just a few short months after President von Hindenburg's death in August 1934, no opposition to the Nazis was to be found. Subsequent ballots and election literature printed only the names of Nazi party officials, and by 1934 most opposition leaders had been rounded up and sent to concentration camps. Control of the press was also crucial. "National Socialism will not repeat the mistakes of prewar Germany, which was unable to put a stop to the maligning of her great essential institutions, army, school, state, etc., and hence broke down in the hour of danger,"[32] declared a Nazi press release in 1934, possibly written by Goebbels. Hitler further emphasized this idea in a 1934 interview: "I shall not tolerate a press the exclusive purpose of which is to destroy what we have undertaken to build up."[33] The media was marshaled to steadfastly support the leader to the exclusion of all other views; as a result, dissent was initially eschewed and ultimately outlawed.

Hitler's deputy Rudolf Hess banned what he called "nimble penmanship," a euphemism for unsanctioned books, brochures, or pamphlets—even those that were sympathetic toward National Socialism. No written or pictorial pieces about the Nazi movement could be published without first passing muster with an official examining commission. These watchdog activities were not solely coordinated through the Promi. Hitler routinely divided and often duplicated responsibilities to ensure the loyalty of Nazi subordinates through competition. Party ideologue Alfred Rosenberg's cultural organizations, notably the Kampfbund für Deutsche Kultur (Combat League for German Culture) and Amt für Kunstpflege (Office for the Cultivation of Art) controlled the content and look of vast amounts of cultural advertising and absorbed a fair share of design production until Goebbels's Promi started flexing its muscles after 1935.

And the Deutsche Arbeitsfront (DAF; German Labor Front), an organization created to replace the trade unions disbanded when the Nazis took control, played a crucial role. Under the watchful eye of Robert Ley, the German Labor Front was in effect responsible for the overall visual style and makeup of the party, and it initiated the publication of a bewildering handbook, the *Organisationsbuch der NSDAP* (Organizational handbook of the National Socialist party).

Published in 1936 with a foreword by Hitler, the *Organisationsbuch* is perhaps the most stupefying Nazi branding document, which lays out the Nazi design strategy schematically and in stultifying detail. It includes organizational charts for every political cell, group, and regional division; each paramilitary organization is defined in detail. It sketches out workers' housing blocks and even designates the house of the superintendent. It is profusely illustrated with color plates that establish the accoutrements of members of the different organizations according to rank: uniforms, symbols, flags, standards, weapons, even belts and satchels. And the back of the book contains chilling informational charts delineating Jewish heredity and the rules of intermarriage.

The oversight of graphic arts was essentially left to the German Labor Front, but surprisingly—especially given the thoroughness of the *Organisationsbuch*— in the end many different governmental bureaus, agencies, and subdivisions independently administered their visual output, from posters to typography. Immediately after the Nazis took control, they published a tidal wave of new laws, both blueprints for Nazi symbols and prohibitions against the abuse of them. These draconian rules forbade misuse of party uniforms and all other party paraphernalia, and only a few companies were licensed to produce official emblems.[34]

Even though national law dictated the size, shape, and positioning of major symbols, flags, and official signs, virtually every organization within

35. *Organisationsbuch der NSDAP* (Organizational handbook of the National Socialist party) Edited in 1936 by the head of the Deutsche Arbeitsfront (DAF; German Labor Front), Dr. Robert Ley, this book continued where *ABC of National Socialism* left off, detailing the organizational principles as well as the graphic identity of the party.

a. Cover
b. Old iteration (left) and new versions (right) of party office signs
c. Special decorations and medals
d. Flags for local divisions of the party
e. Uniforms and accessories for leaders of local groups
f. Medals and insignia

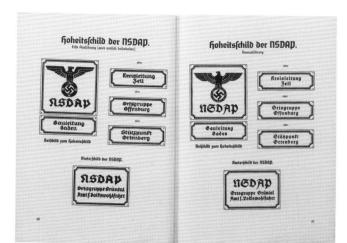

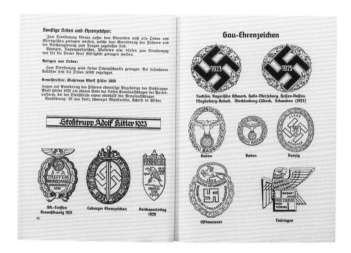

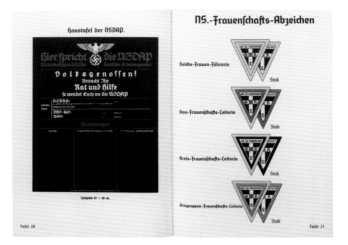

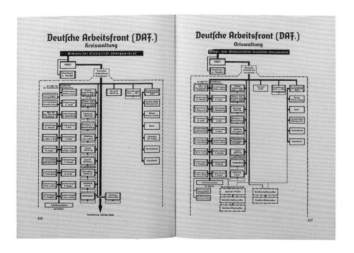

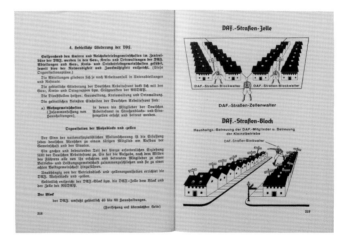

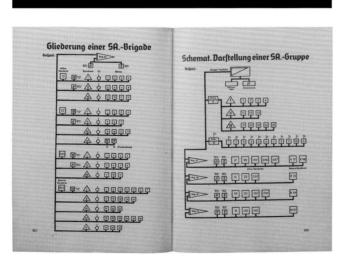

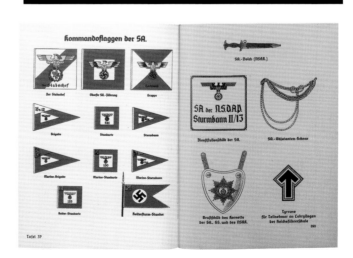

35. *Organisationsbuch der NSDAP* (Organizational handbook of the National Socialist party)

g. Truck pennants for national and local party divisions, and armbands for different organizations
h. Notice board (left page) and woman's league insignia.
i. Organizational hierarchy for the regional and local chapters of the DAF
j. DAF housing block and street plans
k. Organizational hierarchy for SA brigade (left) and platoon (right)
l. Commandership flags for the SA (left); insignia and regalia for the SA (right)

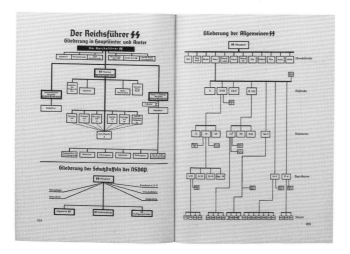

35. *Organisationsbuch der NSDAP* (Organizational handbook of the National Socialist party)

m. Organizational hierarchy for the Reichsführer SS (left) and "regular" SS (right)
n. Epaulets and uniforms for the Hitlerjugend (HJ; Hitler Youth)
o. Flags for the Reichsarbeitsdienstes (Reich Labor Service), an organization created to combat unemployment, whose members served in civic, military, and agricultural construction projects
p–q. Charts showing the Nazi conception of Jewish lineage, with rules of intermarriage between Germans and Jews.

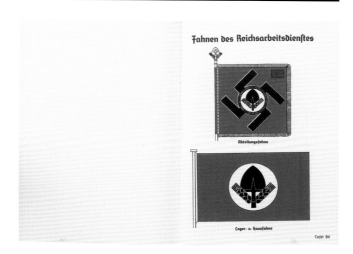

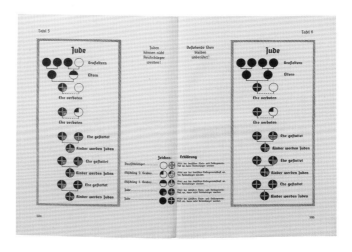

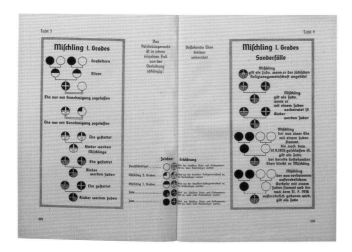

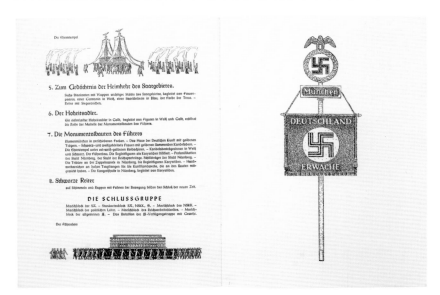

36–37. *Der Weg der NSDAP* (The path of the National Socialist party) This book, produced by the main office of the Reichsführer SS, links the history of the Nazi movement to its iconographic development. 1943

38. *Deutsche Reichspost* (Reich postal service) This poster for the postal service was designed by Ludwig Hohlwein. c. 1935

39. *Die SA, Zeitschrift der Sturmabteilungen der NSDAP* (The SA, journal of the storm troopers of the National Socialist party) The Brownshirts adopted classical symbols, including the Roman dagger and laurel wreath. 1940

40. *Der Hoheitsträger* (The standard bearer) This magazine was published for high party officials and contained important decrees about Nazi iconography. 1938

Background: SA troops from all over Germany rally in Nuremberg, displaying *Deutschland Erwache* standards with individual city names featured on panels below the laurel-wreathed swastikas. c. 1936

the Nazi party (and there were at least fifty at first) dealt with them individually. Every group had its own emblem, a variant on the primary Nazi logo, the swastika. Arrows, lightning bolts, spears, and swords—all symbols of power—were also widely used in Nazi iconography. The SA (Sturmabteilung; storm troopers, aka Brownshirts) incorporated the imperial eagle into their graphic repertoire, which included Roman-style standards topped with the regal bird with talons dug into a laurel-wreathed swastika. Hitler had designed this logo himself for the Nazi newspaper *Völkischer Beobachter* (People's observer), having read in an anti-Semitic tract that the eagle was the "Aryan" of the animal world. The SA adopted an S-shaped arrow that merged into a pointed A. The logo of the German Labor Front included a swastika inside a cogwheel— in its conceptual simplicity it was the quintessence of modernity. The Kraft durch Freude (KDF; Strength through Joy) division of the Labor Front was created to appease dissatisfied workers by organizing cruises and other recreational activities. Its emblem was the DAF logo circled by four propeller blades symbolic of a ship's rotor. The Hitlerjugend (HJ; Hitler Youth) swastika fit perfectly into a diamond shape rather than the usual white disk, and was framed with red-and-white stripes to imbue the symbol with a youthful aura.

The Deutsches Jungvolk (Young People of Germany) adopted a slightly different—darker, more cultish— brand: a white runic sign against a black background.

Graphics were not the only branding tools; the National Socialists became experts in wielding the power of spectacle. Goebbels operated on the premise that the common man is impressed in the long run only by displays of strength and discipline, and Hitler understood the power of size in influencing the masses. This was expressed in the notion that the individual could find identity only through the mass; hence the seemingly endless rows of uniformed followers. It also found form in a Nazi-styled environ- ment of cold, overblown, unadorned structures that were said to represent "Germanness," but were actually designed to assault the mind through their sheer magnitude.

The rally, and later the full-blown political pageant, was carefully orchestrated to trigger a conformist mass response. Before the takeover of power, stage-managed marches of upward of thirty thousand SA frequently surged for as long as five hours, giving the impression of a gigantic movement. Beno von Arent, a theatrical director and later state producer of stage sets, orchestrated and designed the settings for many of the early events, while Hitler's architect,

41. *Kraft durch Freude* (**Strength through Joy**) The Strength through Joy organization replaced trade unions in Nazi Germany. In order to appease unhappy workers, the organization provided perks such as trips and cruises on the Mediterranean, which this postcard commemorates. 1939

42. *Die Deutsche Arbeitsfront. Urlauber Fahrten zur See* (**The German Labor Front. Sea cruise holidays**) Published by the German Labor Front, this program was issued to travelers sent on sea cruises by the Strength through Joy movement. The logos on the flags signify the Nazi party, the German Labor Front, and Strength through Joy. 1939

43. **NSFK** The logo of the Nationalsozialistisches Fliegerkorps (National Socialist Flying Corps) featured an Aryan man with outspread wings. 1939

44. *Kalendar der Deutschen Arbeit* (**German work calendar**) The dagger and the factory smokestacks symbolize the synergy between the Nazi party and the working class. The logo of the German Labor Front, which issued the calendars, is visible in the top left-hand corner. 1941

45. Nazi rally in Nuremberg
Lighting design was used to dramatic effect during these annual late-night rallies. September 1937

Albert Speer, eventually produced and choreographed the huge Nuremberg rallies. Facade was everything. The theaters and halls were routinely draped with slogans set in huge spiky blackletter type; the color red washed over everything. The crowd was usually seated for hours before the processional began. Then came the choreography: first the rank-and-file members took their seats; next the brown-uniformed SA, known as "The Hitlers," took their positions, carrying their standards (they were there both for visual impact and to keep order); then the uniformed party leaders proceeded down a center aisle; finally, Hitler strutted to the stage and gradually assumed the stance of the führer.

Nazi organizers preferred nocturnal events because the masses were more likely to be influenced at night, when the gatherings were more dramatic than in daylight. They arranged cordons of human beings in geometric formations like building blocks. The stage masters' play of light and darkness set to pounding drum music and percussive *Sieg Heil* recitations had the desired hypnotic effect of lulling viewers into a submissive trance. These were not unprecedented techniques; what was new, however, was the intensity and frequency of the public onslaughts.

48   49

46. *Lies auch du den SA-Mann, dein Kamerad im Kleinkrieg des Alltags* (Read the SA-man, your comrade in the small wars of daily life) This poster was designed by Ludwig Hohlwein for the journal *Der SA-Mann* (The SA-man). c. 1940

47–48. *SAKAMPF, S.A.-Kampfspiel* (SA war game) Nazi board game box and figurines. 1933

49. SA pin The SA logo on this collar pin is made of a lightning-bolt S turning into an A. c. 1928

50–52. *Handbuch der SA* (SA handbook) This official guide to SA standards and practices contains photographs and drawings of everything an SA man needs, including instructions for marching and saluting. The methods and means of propaganda are also covered in detailed charts and graphs. 1939

the fist and the face of the nazi brand: the SA and the HJ

The SA was the fist of Nazi propaganda efforts. Hitler saw violence as a critical tool in spreading his influence, and early on he advocated *Saalschlacht* (political brawl) as part of his strategy. To Eugen Hadamovsky, it was the hard sell of Nazi advertising— a flagrant combination of propaganda and terror. Inspired by Mussolini's Blackshirts, Hitler devised a similar sartorial identity for the roughnecks who adhered to his fledgling movement and carried out much of this "guerrilla advertising" in beer cellars and on the street.

The ubiquitous Brownshirts soon became a huge army of order-keepers responsible for protecting Nazi rallies on the one hand and for capturing turf from Communist rivals on the other. In the words of the "Horst Wessel song" (the inflammatory early Nazi anthem written by a Brownshirt later killed by Communists and hailed as a martyr), violence would "free the street for the brown battalions." (The brown shirt became such a potent symbol that brown uniforms were prohibited in 1927—a ban that Nazis easily circumvented by temporarily switching to white shirts; some detachments even stripped down to bare chests or their underwear in a sign of protest.)

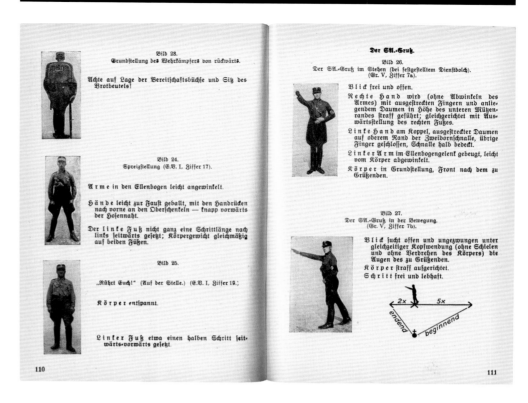

53

54

Reichssporttag des B∙d∙M∙
23∙September∙1934

55

AUSSTELLUNG

hitler-
jungen

FÜR DAS HEER

56

Die Organisation der

Aufbau
Gliederung
Anschriften

At the height of the SA's street influence, a few chosen members were detached to constitute a personal bodyguard called Stoßtrupp Hitler (Hitler Raiding Patrol), which took over close-rank protection duties from the SA. They soon became known as the Schutzstaffel (SS; Protection Squad), and starting in 1929 were headed by Heinrich Himmler. Almost from the beginning this elite corps took on its own symbols and regalia. The smartly tailored black uniform (produced by the German firm Hugo Boss, which also made Wehrmacht uniforms) was designed to distinguish the SS from the rumpled, street-brawling Brownshirts. Their insignia, the SS Sig, was designed in 1931 by Walter Heck, an officer in the SS, who reversed and inverted two Sig runes to create the SS symbol. Apparently, he sold the rights for 2.5 reichsmarks (more than Wilhelm Deffke received for his swastika), and the runic symbol became the ominous insignia of the SS. Brashly flaunting their violent mission, the SS adopted other symbols, such as the death's-head—or skull and crossbones—that derived from eighteenth-century Prussian military regalia.

When Hitler took over the Nazi party, he wasn't initially interested in German adolescents because they could not vote, but Goebbels saw Germany's youth as the key to the Nazis' future. By 1926, when the Hitler Youth was founded, the führer also understood that young people would provide a limitless supply of impressionable followers. The Hitler Youth accepted all Aryan boys, and the Bund Deutscher Mädel (BDM; League of German Girls) all Aryan girls aged fourteen to eighteen (ten- to fourteen-year-old boys belonged to the Deutsches Jungvolk—Young People of Germany—and girls to the Jungmädel—Young Girls). For boys, the Hitler Youth was, in effect, the farm team for the SA, SS, and German Labor Front. There was even a junior Gestapo, the Hitlerjugend Streifendienst (Hitler Youth Patrol Service), which monitored other children. For girls, the organization was a finishing school where they could learn to be loyal wives and fecund

53. Mother medal
Nazis awarded the prestigious Iron Cross and swastika collar pin to women for bearing children for the Reich.
c. 1938

54. *Reichssporttag des BDM* (Sporting day for the League of German Girls)
Poster designed by Ludwig Hohlwein announcing the Bund Deutscher Mädel (BDM) sports day.
1934

55. *Ausstellung Hitlerjungen* (Hitler boys' exhibition)
This poster announces an exhibition of arts and crafts by members of the Hitler Youth.
1943

56. *Die Organisation der HJ* (The organization of the Hitler Youth)
The bold HJ lettering offers a typographic sense of power on the cover of this manual for Hitler Youth members.
c. 1936

57. Sporting event award
Members of the Hitler Youth and League of German Girls were awarded special certificates of merit for taking part in this youth festival.
1934

Background (top):
Members of the BDM marching in their exercise clothes.
July 1929

Background (bottom):
Hitler Youth salute during Hitler speech at Nuremberg rally.
1937

57

Deutsches Jugendfest 1934

Bei den sportlichen Wettkämpfen am 23 Juni 1934 errang einen Sieg im Dreikampf mit 52 PH. Hans Weikert

Als Anerkennung verleihen wir diese Urkunde

Reichsjugendführer
Reichssportführer

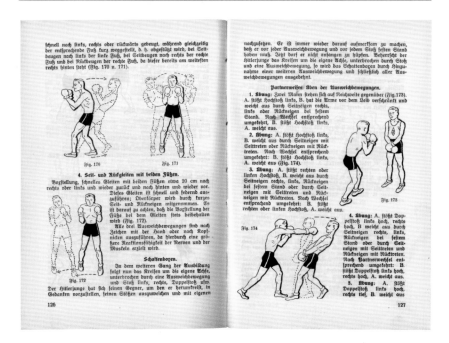

58–59. *H.J. im Dienst*
(Hitler Youth in service)
The handbook for
Hitler Youth members
covered everything
from boxing and
shooting to camping
and cooking. The
diamond surrounding
the swastika distin-
guished the Hitler Youth
from the older party
organization.
1938

60. *Postmerkbuch für
den Schulunterricht*
(Postal system
explained in school)
This school manual
was published by the
Reichspostministerium
(Postal Ministry) to
teach the efficiency of
the system.
1939

Background:
Deutsches Jungvolk
(Young People
of Germany) in
an open-air camp
near Berlin.
c. 1935

mothers. The members wore snappy uniforms, went on overnight hikes, played sports, and earned badges—lots of badges. They spent most of their time at camps with minimal parental control, learning the Nazi creed, which included honor, sacrifice, camaraderie, and anti-Semitism. They canvased neighborhoods, distributed leaflets, recruited new members, and often engaged in violent skirmishes with Communist youths. When the Nazis came to power in 1933, both youth groups grew in size from thousands of members to millions, and by 1936 all young German "Aryans" were required to join the Nazi organization. During the Allied bombardments of Germany in 1944, Hitler Youth members manned antiaircraft guns.

Much of the Hitler Youth's fervency came from the barrage of signs and symbols designed to instill conceit and affiliation in their vulnerable minds. Banners, pennants, and flags were carried with pride by members of the Hitler Youth Bann, their version of a military regiment. Each unit carried a striped red-and-white flag that featured a yellow scroll above a black eagle, emblazoned with a swastika, grasping in its talons a white sword and black hammer. The Deutsches Jungvolk flagpoles were of polished black wood with a white metal bayonet finial, while their

flags were emblazoned with a single lightning bolt rune—as though to say they were just one rune away from the SS. Each element was carefully designed to bring pride to members of the Hitler Youth or League of German Girls as they became part of the Nazi brand, while ultimately propagating the image of the perfect Aryan.

Postmerkbuch
für den Schulunterricht

Herausgegeben vom Reichspostministerium
Berlin, Januar 1939

61

62

wielding graphics

nazi type: a gothic tale

The Nazis politicized art and nationalized aesthetics in an attempt to control all aspects of German life. In this endeavor, no detail was too minute, no facet of everyday existence too mundane to be controlled. Much of it was simply the quotidian work of producing the identity materials for the state and party, and all output was rigorously scrutinized to ensure strict conformity with the Nazi visual identity. Type was deemed critical; it was examined as much for its readability—and even its aesthetics—as for its Germanic origins.

Despite Hitler's personal influence on graphics, the style ultimately appropriated by the Nazis resulted from fierce debates that raged inside the party during its rise to power between champions of *Völkism* (the revival of Teutonic traditions) and proponents of modernism (those who embraced Expressionism and Bauhaus ideas). Indeed, the Nazi rejection of modernism was not immediate, even though modernists in Germany, including the Bauhaus, were ideologically associated with left-wing parties (and seen as Jewish sympathizers by right-wing anti-Semites). There was prolonged disagreement within the Nazi party regarding which style would best distinguish the new Germany from the old. When Hitler came to power, the conservatives took for granted that their historical Germanicism would become the country's official style, while others who leaned toward modernism presumed that the Nazi revolution would emulate Italian Fascism in adopting the new style. They believed that a new kind of art should have its place in the New Order. But although Nazi style was never entirely purged of modernist influences, the *Völkists* won, and a retrograde style inveigled its way into society. Gothic (or blackletter) became the preferred typeface, while more modern sans serif faces were rejected.

To practice graphic design and typography under Nazi auspices, designers were compelled to join trade chambers and adhere to their regulations. The aesthetic guidelines dictated not only how Nazi and government documents should look, but even how lettering for unofficial use must conform. Control was exercised and had an impact on every calligrapher, type designer, and graphic designer working in a Third Reich "creative" office, agency, or studio.

There was no central office of type doctrine, however, so decisions were ultimately left to minor bureaucrats who had to guess at Hitler's desires and interpret his rambling pronouncements. (For example, he warned against the "spoilers of art": the Cubists, Futurists, Dadaists, and other avant-gardists.) Although different ministries established their own styles within basic prescriptions, the German Labor Front, which controlled the trade chambers in charge of printing and typography, was responsible for

61. Schwabacher lettering
Schwabacher was an officially sanctioned Nazi typeface, but by 1941 it had been condemned as Jewish lettering.
c. 1937

62. *Wesen, Grundsätze und Ziele der N.S.D.A.P.* (Essence, principles, and goals of the National Socialist party)
This Nazi program by party ideologue Alfred Rosenberg uses a version of blackletter.
1935

Background:
Nazi election posters in Berlin reveal a range of sanctioned typographic styles.
1932

65

66

67

68

developing graphic teaching materials and produced annual type-specimen books featuring a limited number of presumably sanctioned typefaces—most of which were variations on the Gothic Fraktur.

Verboten were typefaces designed by Jews and other "cultural Bolsheviks." (Lucian Bernhard's typefaces, for example, were denigrated because he was thought to be a Jew, although he was not.) Alfred Rosenberg, head of the Office for the Supervision of the Entire Cultural and Ideological Education and Training of the NSDAP, was one of the leading advocates of *Völkism*. In one of his bombastic 1933 editorials in the *Völkischer Beobachter*, he railed: "A bitter and systematic resistance has been organized against the New National Socialist ideal of a spiritually healthy art anchored in the race."[35] He condemned the Nazi student association and its supporters who sought to adopt modernist forms and opposed the *völkisch* old guard. They insisted that *Völkism* was kitsch, and considered Gothic typefaces such as Fraktur and Schwabacher to be part of the antiquated past. Paul Renner, designer of the quintessentially modern Futura, who wrote a book titled *Kulturbolschewismus?* (Cultural Bolshevism) that attacked Nazi anti-Semitism and medievalism in art, found unexpected allies in these Nazi modernists. But ultimately they lost their struggle.

Hitler's adoption of *Völkism* was a strategy calculated to engage the worker and peasant classes in the Nazis' early mission to attract rural votes.

63–68. Gothic lettering
The Nazis politicized the use of Gothic lettering by claiming nationalist origins for it. Portfolios like this one, designed by Prof. P. Hampel, targeting advertising designers, offered hand-produced stylistic variations on the basic Fraktur. c. 1938

69–72. Lettering samples
This selection, designed by Wilhelm Dechert (69), Alfred Spantig (70, 72), and Von Richmann (71), included blackletter (also known as German lettering) as well as a sans serif brush letter. c. 1938

Gothic typefaces—including spiky Fraktur, the more rounded Schwabacher, Textura, and Rotunda, which had appeared in Germany during the thirteenth century and was therefore considered to be historically pure—were allegedly imbued with *völkist* symbolism. Here again the Nazis were perpetuating a tradition started during the nineteenth century by earlier German racialists who had appropriated Gothic style and declared it Teutonic. Of course, the international origins of Gothic art were ignored in the Nazis' fervent embrace of their exclusionary mythology (just as

they ignored the swastika's complex historical roots). Because Gothic type had been preserved as a text face mostly in central and northern European countries throughout the nineteenth century, the Nazis contended that it was "Germanic."

Rejection of "non-Germanic" alphabets from commercial and government printing was a recurring theme in Rosenberg's cultural propaganda from 1933 to 1935. His campaign to stamp out non-German lettering featured stickers with slogans admonishing citizens to use only Gothic-style letters, or *deutsche*

Schrift (German lettering; also referred to as *schöne deutsche Schrift*, or "beautiful German script"), the designated type for the German nation. A leader in this campaign was *Die zeitgemäße Schrift* (Contemporary lettering), a journal devoted to type, which regularly sponsored German script competitions among art students. In a 1935 editorial titled "Writing and Lettering in the Service of the New State," the editors of *Die zeitgemäße Schrift* explained:

> [Our] new conception of the State, which claims as its own all the phenomena of racial life, is definitely concerned with the training of the growing generation; moreover, the system of education and instruction, newly reorganized by the State, is forced to utilize all measures and possibilities which may serve to put the new ideas into practice.... Among such education measures special attention to writing and lettering is included, and certain indications permit us to recognize that the interest of the State in both these important branches of instruction is increasing.[36]

Alongside its regular diet of Fraktur, Schwabacher, Rotunda, and Kanzlei typefaces, *Die zeitgemäße Schrift* occasionally exhibited samples of sans serif lettering and calligraphy. The editors published a few laudatory articles on Rudolf Koch, designer of Kabel, and Peter Behrens, whom Hitler admired as the father of the AEG's new corporate identity. But the journal usually did not stray too far from the party line, promoting blackletter as the preeminent German face.

In 1935 Hitler shocked ardent proponents of *Völkism* when he unexpectedly declared that, just as modern art was "degenerate," the Gothic arts so beloved by "petrified backward-lookers" were "dangers to National Socialism." He suddenly railed against those who established "railroad stations in

73–79. TYPO:
Typographisches Skizzieren und Drucksachenentwerfen
(TYPO: Typographic sketching and printed matter design)
This graphic manual, published by the German Labor Front, featured new sanctioned letterforms, including Fraktur (77), Rotunda (78) and Paul Renner's Futura (79). c. 1938

original German Renaissance style, street signs and typewriter keyboards with genuine Gothic letters."[37] Underscoring that idea, Hadamovsky warned that "a spirit of superficial and sentimental patriotism [*patriotischer Kitsch*] has often poisoned and spoiled the arts and crafts with its flat and uninspired, if well-meant, approach."[38] Consequently, a new style of Gothic typefaces appeared, in which traditional forms were simplified to be readable while still conforming to the overall Nazi style. These typefaces, marketed by type foundries to play on nationalistic sensibilities, were named Grosse Deutschland (great Germany), National, and Deutschland. These typefaces monumentalized Gothic forms, much as Albert Speer's and Paul L. Troost's Nazi architecture transfigured classicism. The new direction was immediately implemented in the German Labor Front's first instructional type book, *TYPO: Typographisches Skizzieren und Drucksachenentwerfen* (TYPO: Typographic sketching and printed matter design), which included Antiqua and Grotesk, as well as Paul Renner's Futura.[39]

"To be German means to be clear!"[40] Hitler said, which to him meant infused with political purpose. Anything that might be confusing, including typography, endangered the political program. So a significant shift in policy started in the precincts of graphic design, and although blackletter was never entirely rejected, it was eventually marginalized. On 3 January 1941, Hitler's lieutenant Martin Bormann issued the following directive:

> To consider or to designate the so-called Gothic script as a German script is wrong: the so-called Gothic script consists of Schwabacher-Jewish letters. Exactly as they later on took possession of the newspapers, so the Jews residing in Germany took possession of the printing shops when printing was introduced and thus came about in Germany

80–81. *Die Deutsche Polizei* (The German police)
This magazine devoted to the police illustrates the shift from reliance on blackletter in 1937 (80) to Antiqua in 1943 (81). 1937–43

82–85. Portfolio of Hitler quotes and Nazi slogans
"One people, one empire, one leader" (82); "Only those who are strong enough to claim their freedom are free" (83); "People are liberated not through inaction but through sacrifice!" (84); "Germany must live even if we must die" (85). 1938–40

the strong introduction of the Schwabacher-Jewish letters.

On this day in a conference with Mr. Reichsleiter Amann and printing plant owner Adolf Mueller, the führer has decided that Roman type shall from now on be designated as the normal type. Gradually all printing products shall be adjusted to this normal type. As soon as this is possible textbook-wise, in the village schools and the elementary schools only Roman shall be taught.

By order of the führer Mr. Reichsleiter Amann will proceed to change over to normal script those newspapers and magazines which already have a foreign circulation or foreign circulation of which is desirable.[41]

One reason for this shift in policy was Goebbels's fear that Fraktur type—admittedly difficult to read—would compromise foreign propaganda campaigns, which at this point, nearly a year before Pearl Harbor and before the attack on Soviet Russia, were given high ministerial priority. Another rationale was that German pilots found it difficult to read when used as markings on airplanes. Furthermore, the official signs in occupied lands required a more universal type solution. The use of Fraktur was impeding the plan of world domination, and so—with their usual efficiency—the Nazis moved summarily to a new graphic scheme.

nazi linguistics: the creative word

In his treatise *Propaganda and National Power*, Eugen Hadamovsky devotes one chapter to "The Creative Word." He says: "The word is equally capable of conveying truth or falsehood, and man alone can determine how to use it."[42] He goes on to explain that part of the Nazi revolution was to pit new words against old: the impetuous terminology of political propaganda versus the refined language of diplomacy. Under the Nazis, jargon and euphemism were integral to building the Nazi identity. Ultimately they were also integral to the policy of genocide.

"In the field of political propaganda the creation of catchphrases and slogans had been developed to perfection long before our time. The battle cry of a movement has always been the most effective of any propaganda,"[43] wrote Hadamovsky. The German nation in World War I, he added, was not beaten on the battlefield, but lost the war of words—the absence of an effective slogan left the people with broken spirits. So official catchphrases like *Deutschland erwache* (Germany awake) and *Ein Volk, ein Reich, ein Führer* (One people, one empire, one leader), or even the word *Ja!* (Yes) when juxtaposed with Hitler's portrait, were integral to the mind-infiltrating branding campaign.

The telegraphing of meaning through abbreviation was also part of the Nazi strategy of inclusion and exclusion; creative spellings beckon those in the know even while obstructing the uninitiated. Meant as codes for members of the Nazi party, the new enigmatic coinages often stood for National Socialist organizations or groups, or gave new titles for old jobs; they gave the insider a sense of belonging. The initials SA provide a case in point: they could easily be construed as *Saalschutzabteilung* (assembly hall protection) or *Sportsabteilung* (sports team), but very rapidly became universally recognized as the name of the Sturmabteilung (Storm Troopers). The use of initials or abbreviations for the SA, SS, and Gestapo (Geheime Staatspolizei, or National Secret Police) became part of the branding strategy. "Each one, by its mere existence, represents propaganda and a spiritual chain; its mere mention arouses positive or negative reactions,"[44] said Hadamovsky, noting that certain words, like visual symbols, were impossible to "eradicate" after becoming part of the vernacular. Abbreviation takes the tangle out of tongue-twisting words and titles; they can make something more friendly than it is—or more threatening than it might be.[45] Kripo, the abbreviation for the Nazi Kriminalpolizei (Criminal Police) takes an inauspicious term and enshrouds it in mystery. On the other hand, BDM sounds somewhat more impressive than the Bund Deutscher Mädel (League of German Girls), a young girls' organization. All these sub-brand names of the Nazi über-brand contribute to the illusion of a vast centrally controlled network that inspires either confidence or fear (and sometimes both). And of course the term *Nazi* itself derived from the first two syllables of Nationalsozialistische Deutsche Arbeiterpartei (as pronounced in German: Na and zi), the National Socialist party.

the poster as weapon

In the Nazi branding campaign, posters played a crucial role. Interestingly, in his detailed analysis for Nazi propagandists, *Das politische Plakat* (The political poster), Erwin Schockel argued against promulgating

a particular poster style, as it would limit the options for communicating to the largest constituency. The poster, he argued, is not an end in itself but serves the political message. Individual artists brought their own styles to the form, which were, he noted, "pragmatically eclectic." Mjölnir (aka Hans Schweitzer), Theo Matejko, and Franz O. Schiffers, the leading Nazi graphic artists, were ostensibly "assistants" to the propaganda visionaries, and their work served the needs of the party fully—alleged creative individuality was simply a tool to be used toward this aim. Still, the development of poster campaigns as part of a larger propaganda effort was to be viewed as a kind of art. "Great propagandists are just as unique as great artists," wrote Schockel. "They are the shining example for the many who faithfully strive to fulfill their duty as helpers of the great men, as the latter pursue the role that fate has allotted to them."[46]

The first Nazi visual campaign took place in 1926, when Hitler was forbidden to make public speeches in Bavaria (and soon in most other German states) after his release from prison. The Nazis seized the opportunity. An action committee was formed to protest the ban, and the party followed up with a sucessful campaign. On Hitler's birthday, 20 April, the Nazi party launched a series of posters featuring a flattering portrait of Hitler with two bandages across his mouth inscribed with the word *Redeverbot* (ban on speaking). The posters had different subheadings. One read: "He alone among 2,000 million people on earth is not allowed to speak in Germany!" Rather than thwart the party's attempts at rabble-rousing, the ban gave the Nazis an opportunity to demonstrate their propaganda skills.

Some posters were astoundingly modern, and one image stands out above all others: a 1932 election poster so minimalist that it could easily be confused with a modernist design.[47] The black-and-white poster features Hitler's face (just a head without neck or shoulders) against a stark black background. Its simple caption-headline, "Hitler," is set in unusual white

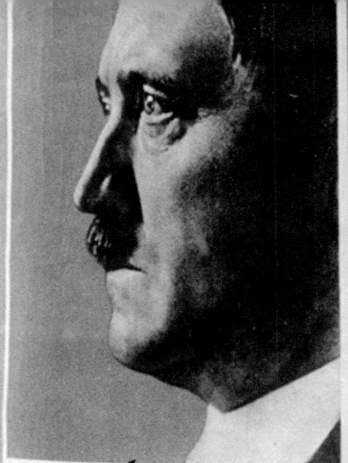

Ein Volk - ein Reich - ein Führer!

86

87

88

sans serif capital letters. The only typographical tic is a seemingly superfluous square over the *I* (perhaps a visual pun on his famously cropped mustache). "The calmness, goodness and strength that radiate from Hitler's face communicate themselves to the observer," wrote Schockel in *Das politische Plakat*. "The impression it makes on people of unspoilt mind must be powerful. In addition, we had the poster printed on a black background which at the time served as an eye-catcher in the midst of the otherwise garish colors of advertising pillars."[48] The Nazis were pleased with the results. During the 1933 election, Goebbels exclaimed: "Our placards have become wonderful. The propaganda is being carried out in the best possible manner. The whole country has to pay attention."[49]

In the early years, Hitler and Goebbels designed posters themselves, devising their own symbols and slogans. These posters echoed the aggressiveness of the movement in constructing stereotypes and tapping into popular emotions. They capitalized on unemployment, crime, and anti-Semitism. Some were cautionary: *Unsere letzte Hoffnung: Hitler* (Our last hope: Hitler); others were commanding: *Wacht auf! Und wählt den völkischen Block* (Wake up! Vote for the National Block). While some posters had simple messages and clear slogans, many others were intended to provide information that could not easily be disseminated otherwise. The poster was more than a branding tool; it became a means of communication.

Posters created before the Nazis' seizure of power in 1933 largely comprised action scenes. This particular characteristic distinguished the Nazis from most other Weimar parties, although Communist posters used just as much action (the Nazis even appropriated some of the Communist imagery, including the breaking of chains and lock-jawed soldiers fighting the political foe). The rhetoric was fairly obvious: fists slamming down on government leaders, official buildings, and other left-wing enemies; angry SA poised for attack; corpulent Jews counting their profits. The drawings by

89. *Dreissig Kriegsartikel für das deutsche Volk* (Thirty war articles for the German people)
The cover of this incendiary pamphlet by Joseph Goebbels, in which he describes the war as self-defense and the mere thought of capitulation as high treason, was illustrated by Mjölnir.
1943

90. Ban on speaking
For a brief time during the 1920s Hitler was forbidden to address public meetings in much of Germany. This poster was part of a succesful Nazi campaign to exploit censureship of Hitler.
1926

91. *Sieg über Versailles* (Victory over Versailles)
Hitler rose to power promising to end the harsh penalties imposed on Germany by the Allies in the Treaty of Versailles, which ended World War I. Poster designed by Dassel.
1939

92. *Mander s'ischt Zeit!* (Men, the time has come!)
This anti-Semitic postcard, designed by Frank Köck, calls to chase Jews out of Austria following the Anschluss (annexation).
1938

Mjölnir expressed the power of the movement through a sketchy crayon style that was at once immediate and heroic. His 1932 *Schluss jetzt! Wählt Hitler* (Enough now! Vote Hitler) shows a herculean, bare-chested figure, wearing a swastika belt buckle, forcefully breaking the chains of republican oppression.

Posters were initially hung on whatever pillars or walls could be commandeered; eventually, glass cases were mounted in all cities for mandatory indoor and outdoor postings. Once in power, the Promi established the German Propaganda Studio to produce the majority of state posters. Goebbels believed that high quality could be achieved only by a subsidized professional studio, and he rejected requests by other departments and field offices of the ministry to design their own work. The rationale was that the finances were not available—and the designers not good enough—to maintain the desired standards

across the board. The Propaganda Studio was therefore responsible for considerable output, including a series of wall posters that began in the early 1940s called the "Weekly Motto of the NSDAP," which included slogans excerpted from texts or speeches, intended as morale-building bromides targeted at factories and other workplaces.

As the rhetoric of the master race and Aryan superman became shrill in the mid-1930s, the style of Heroic Realism (or what might be called National Socialist Realism) came to dominate Nazi poster art. The stylization against which Schockel had warned took over the later posters. The "wretchedly heroic posters," as critics referred to them, all started to look very much alike. One of the artists responsible for these heroic clichés—although his work was technically far superior to that of most other poster artists of the day—was Ludwig Hohlwein, whose style—generally

93. *Ganz Deutschland hört den Führer mit dem Volksempfänger* (All Germany hears the führer with the people's radio) The Nazis dubbed their own line of radios *Volksempfänger,* "people's radio." This photomontage designed by Leonid suggests that the medium and the leader are one and the same. 1936

94. *Gebt mir 4 Jahre Zeit* (Give me 4 years' time) This photomontage starkly establishes the hierarchy of Nazi icons. 1937

95. *Auch hier liegt unser Lebensraum!* (Here also is our living space!) This postcard suggests the Nazis' intention to colonize Africa. The countries highlighted in red on the African continent refer to the former colonies that Germany lost following its defeat in World War I. c. 1933

96. *Arbeit und Brot durch den Nationalsozialismus Liste 1* (Work and bread through National Socialist List 1) This 1932 election poster used uncharacteristically economical graphic forms (actually more consistent with the swastika's simplicity) to convey a modern rather than *völkisch* message. 1932

termed *Hohlweinstil*—dominated German advertising throughout the late 1920s, 1930s, and into the 1940s. His depictions of Hitler Youth and the SS were given monumental stances and lit to accentuate their grandeur. His work did not demonize; his role was to mythologize. An early member of the party, Hohlwein stated in a 1933 issue of *Gebrauchsgraphik* (Applied graphic design), how art must operate in the service of the nation:

Today, art, as a cultural factor, is more than ever called upon to take a leading place in building up and conserving cultural values. It must take its place in the front ranks of the legion, which Europe has gathered to preserve her individuality against the onslaughts from the East. Art is the best possible disturbing agent for ideas and intellectual tendencies. Commercial art is doubly effective in this sense for it stands in the very forefront, giving form and expression to the daily panorama and forcibly dominating even those who would ordinarily remain impervious to artistic influences. May the best among us realize fully the significance of what is at stake and their own responsibility and labor creatively, and with conviction work at the preservation of our cultural civilization and its restoration to perfectly healthy conditions.[50]

Hohlwein did set a standard against which Nazi poster iconography must be judged. It is incorrect to say definitively that Hohlwein invented National Socialist Realism, but his work was the paradigm.

culture war

spreading anti-semitism

Nazi propaganda was largely shaped by two overlapping narratives: German superiority and the goal of world domination was tied to the defamation and ultimate eradication of all opponents. The Jews bore the brunt of what might be called branding demonization, which was communicated through all the media at Hitler's disposal, notably the party newspaper. "If one can judge the value of a newspaper by the hatred of its enemies, then [the *Völkischer Beobachter*] was the most valuable paper in Germany,"[51] Hitler wrote. The *Völkischer Beobachter* (People's observer) was a little-read anti-Semitic paper from Munich, which Hitler bought in 1920 to become the voice of the National Socialist party. The newspaper was suspended a few times in the early 1920s for attacks on the Weimar government and anti-Semitic articles, but, with Dietrich Eckart (an early party member and participant in the Munich Putsch) and Alfred Rosenberg as its editors, it maintained its anti-Semitic thrust and became the instrument of Nazi propaganda until the end of World War II. In 1926 the Nazi party began publishing another newspaper, the *Illustrierter Beobachter* (Illustrated observer). Following in a long tradition of German illustrated weeklies, the paper was intended less as a party organ than as a popular tabloid— short on in-depth journalism but long on innuendo— that purported to offer news sandwiched between stories on the rise of National Socialism and dollops of scandalous gossip.

But the most foul of the Nazi press (and during the period of the Third Reich hundreds of defamatory papers were published) was a privately run weekly called *Der Stürmer* (The stormer), edited by the rabid Jew-baiter Julius Streicher. The journal's prominently typeset motto, *Die Juden sind unser Unglück!* (The Jews are our misery), flagrantly announced its content full of fantastical stories about fabricated crimes by Jews, including ritual murder and savage rape. A semi-official organ of the Nazis, *Der Stürmer* was published for twenty-two years—right up to the final weeks of the Third Reich—and its sole purpose was to slander the German Jewish population. Its message was conveyed through hideous pornographic depictions and gross caricatures of Jews. At its height, *Der Stürmer* printed over two million copies per week, and the paper was posted in public display cases in every German town and city, but its circulation began to plummet around 1940, when Jews were eliminated from every walk of German life—in a sense it fell victim to its own success.

Streicher also published anti-Semitic children's books, notably *Der Giftpilz* (The poisonous mushroom) and *Trau keinem Fuchs auf grüner Heid und keinem Jud bei seinem Eid!* (Trust no fox on the green heath and no Jew upon his oath). Aimed at children, these books laid out preposterous lies designed to justify anti-Semitic

97. *Völkischer Beobachter* (People's observer) Advertisement for the official Nazi newspaper. While covering news of the party, it was also a clarion of anti-Semitic rhetoric. 1932

98. *Der Stürmer* (The stormer) The rabidly anti-Semitic weekly, edited by Julius Streicher, was replete with bloodcurdling scandal. Its motto, "The Jews Are Our Misery," became synonymous with Nazi policy. 1941

99. *Der Jude in Polen* (The Jew in Poland) This supplement to *Der Stürmer* attacked the Jewish population in occupied Poland. The traditional design of the newspaper framed inflammatory photographs. c. 1939

Background: Anti-Semitic demonstrators organized by the Nazis picket a Jewish shop in Berlin. 1933

policy. *Der Giftpilz* was a monstrosity that reviled Jews, explaining how they had insinuated themselves into German society, and how to recognize them. One chapter vituperates, "How to Tell a Jew: The Jewish nose is bent. It looks like the number six."

Der Angriff (The attack), Goebbels's own newspaper, was slightly more sophisticated in concept and look than *Der Stürmer,* though it was no less incendiary. Slanderous attacks on Jewish members of the Weimar establishment were common, as were scabrous cartoons by one of the Nazis' more effective poster artists: Mjölnir, whose pseudonym refers to Thor's hammer in Nordic mythology, which also became a symbol of Germanic neopaganism. The word comes from "pulverize," which suited the artist's treatment of his subject. Hundreds of other Nazi newspapers and magazines eventually filled the newsstands throughout Germany.

Hitler loved films, and Goebbels made cinema one of the most valued tools in his media arsenal. When, in the late 1920s, Hitler allied himself with the influential media magnate Alfred Hugenberg—who owned the right-wing Scherl Verlag and various newspapers and wire services, as well as the prestigious UFA film company—he ensured that Nazi ideology would be visible in cinemas nationwide. The epic films by Leni Riefenstahl, the German actress turned director, were paradigms of heroic branding propaganda. In *Triumph des Willens* (Triumph of the will, 1934) she created, through innovative camera angles and editing, a vivid cinematic monument to the leader of the state and the masses who served it. Her skill with the camera and her artistic vision made her Hitler's favorite propagandist. Later Riefenstahl films, including *Tag der Freiheit: Unsere Wehrmacht* (Day of freedom: Our armed forces, 1935) and *Olympia* (1938), were feature-length kinetic posters that profoundly contributed to the branding effort.

The Nazis also resorted to exhibitions as a means to promote their image of the New Germany.

100–102. *Der Giftpilz* (The poisonous mushroom) Illustrated by Philipp Rupprecht and published by Der Stürmer Verlag, this children's book was among the most scurrilous anti-Semitic publications of the era. It is the story of a German mother explaining to her child how mushrooms are like people, some good and others poisonous. Over 64 pages the book compares Jews to poisonous mushrooms, and explains why no good German should have to tolerate the presence of Jews in Germany. 1938

103–105. *Trau keinem Fuchs auf grüner Heid und keinem Jud bei seinem Eid!* (Trust no fox on the green heath and no Jew upon his oath) Written by a grade school teacher, Elvira Bauer, illustrated by Philipp Rupprecht, and published by Der Stürmer Verlag, this anti-Semitic book aimed at children was widely distributed in preschools and kindergartens. The title was based on an anti-Semitic slogan dating back to the fifteenth century. 1936

106

107

108

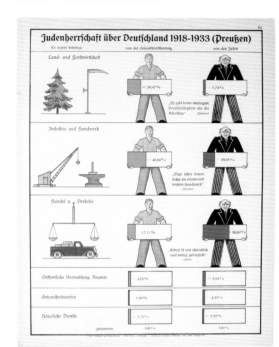

109

110

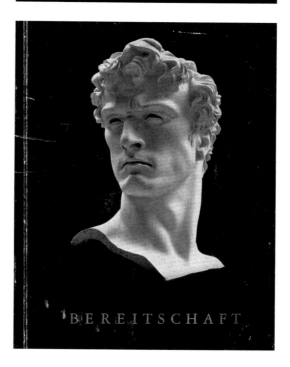

BEREITSCHAFT

HEFT 2 · FEBRUAR 1940 · 8. JAHRGANG · POSTVERSANDORT LEIPZIG   25 PFG.

106–10. Classroom posters
Anti-Semitism was rampant throughout the Nazi school system. Using pseudoscientific means and pictorial manipulation, these classroom wall charts and graphs warn against the dangers of mixed breeding (106, 109); the relative productive worth of Jewish businesses compared to German labor (107); the comparative physical traits of German and Jewish children (108); and the virtues of being a stalwart German (110). c. 1938

111–12. *Bereitschaft* (Readiness) nude sculpture and bust
Arno Breker's sculptures glorified the Aryan characteristics favored by the Nazis. Many of his works were displayed in front of Nazi buildings. 1937, 1939

113. *Neues Volk* (New people)
The photograph on the cover of this popular Nazi periodical emphasizes the Aryan physical ideal. 1940

114. *Deutsches Volk Deutsche Arbeit* (German people German labor) This catalog cover designed by Herbert Bayer (who later emigrated to the United States) shows scant Nazi iconography, though it is nonetheless present inside the book. The exhibition was designed as a showplace for German products and culture. 1934

115. Lufthansa advertising This advertisement designed by Kurt Wendt promotes commercial flights to Düsseldorf for one of the many Nazi cultural exhibitions. 1937

116. *Grosse deutsche Kunstausstellung* (Great German art exhibition) The exhibition of German art organized by the Nazis was held every year, starting in 1937. This image, designed by Richard Klein, was featured on all the posters for the annual exhibition. It reveals the political underpinnings of the art. 1938

117. *Entartete Kunst* (Degenerate art) This poster was not for the famous *Entartete Kunst* exhibition, but for a smaller exhibition of "Bolshevik and Jewish cultural documents" held in March 1936. Designed by Hans Vitus Vierthaler, it is intended to ridicule a painting by El Lissitsky. 1936

They produced exhibitions such as *Schaffendes Volk* (A nation at work), which promoted the Nazis' four-year plan for economic self-sufficiency and urged the public to buy German goods, and *Die Küche—Das Reich der Frau* (The kitchen: The woman's domain). Many exhibitions were designed to demonize the Nazis' declared enemies: *Der ewige Jude* (The eternal Jew*)* and *Der Bolschewismus* (Bolshevism) were both held in 1937. They were organized by various government bureaus, including the Institut für Deutsche Kultur- und Wirtschaftspropaganda (Institute for German Culture and Advertising Propaganda) and the Amt für Ausstellungs- und Messewesen (Office for Exhibitions and Trade Show Fairs). Herbert Bayer, the Bauhaus teacher and art director of the Dorland advertising agency, who eventually fled Nazi Germany, designed catalogs for a few of the more notable exhibitions, where he mixed a modern style with a traditional nationalist aesthetic. Among these were *Deutsches Volk Deutsche Arbeit* (German people German labor) of 1934, *Das Wunder des Lebens* (The wonder of life) of 1935, and the *Deutschland* exhibition of 1936.

The catalog cover for *Deutschland* was rendered in the sleek airbrushed technique that Bayer used for his commercial advertising and magazine covers—a style that was neither Bauhaus nor National Socialist Realism, but used smooth airbrush renderings in a modern decorative manner.

The famous *Entartete Kunst* (Degenerate art) exhibition opened in Munich in 1937 to coincide with the first *Grosse deutsche Kunstausstellung* (Great German art exhibition), which featured art by approved German artists and was mounted at the Haus der Deutschen Kunst (House of German art) to inaugurate this first Nazi public works project, designed by architect Paul L. Troost. The *Entartete Kunst* exhibition was designed to turn public opinion against modernism. Hitler's bêtes noires covered progressive modern movements such as Expressionism, Cubism, Dada, the New Objectivity, and, of course, the Bauhaus. Few artists working in these genres were unscathed. Even though only six of the artists were Jewish, Nazi slogans strewn across the walls, such as "Revelation of the Jewish Racial Soul,"

were often anti-Semitic. The works in the show were
hung with accompanying texts that attacked the
art and artists. As described by Hitler, "degenerate"
art was painting and sculpture that was an insult
to "German feeling" and that in his view lacked artistic
skill. The show attracted huge crowds in the various
German and Austrian cities where it toured, and it
became the most well-attended avant-garde exhibition
of the century.

Once the Nazi brand was well established in
Germany, the next stage was selling a sympathetic yet
forceful image abroad. The Nazis used propaganda
to try to make the new regime acceptable to foreign
governments. The Nazi export had to be unwavering
yet palatable to non-Nazis. Positive depictions of
the regime were issued abroad through newsreels
and magazine articles. In addition to Goebbels and
Hadamovsky, Hitler's old friend and "press secretary"
Ernst "Putzi" Hanfstängel, an affable multilinguist
who enjoyed good relations with many reporters,
attempted to put a favorable face on the Third Reich's
ambitions while touting the führer's successful
renewal of the German economy. The more deplorable
aspects of the totalitarian internal policy were ignored.

branding the unnameable

The relentless anti-Semitic campaigns ultimately
reached a previously unimaginable nadir: the
systematic extermination of the Jewish population.
The offensive to discredit Jews had been strategically
planned (much of it by the Promi), and the steady
torrent of rabid anti-Semitic words and pictures—
newspapers, exhibitions, films, books, posters—had
an incalculable influence on the public. By the time
the Final Solution was presented, behind closed
doors, to top Nazi officials by Reinhard Heydrich at
the Wannsee Conference in Berlin on 20 January 1942,
the campaign against Jews—the visual, verbal, and
physical assaults—had achieved the desired effect and

118. Stickers
These small sheets
printed with Hitler
slogans and anti-Semitic
slander were pasted
to the backs of postal
envelopes. They were
produced cheaply
in large numbers by
the NSDAP in Munich.
1941–42

**119–20. Little Certificate
of Heredity**
This document gene-
rated by the Nazi party
in Vienna establishes
the heredity of its owner.
The option "German
blooded (Aryan)" is
underlined.
1941

Background:
Following its annexation
of Austria, Germany
lost little time in
Nazifying that land.
On this typical Vienna
street, a notice posted
on the shop window
ends with the words
"Jews not welcome."
March 1938

perverted the minds of many. Ghetto liquidations and summary executions in concentration camps became more frequent, and news of them, despite the Nazis' efforts to keep them secret, was leaking out to the public and media.

One of the cruelest Nazi slogans was the beguiling promise *Arbeit macht frei* (Work will set you free), which was posted at the entrance to several concentration camps. In 1872 the German nationalist Lorenz Diefenbach had titled his novel about a man who finds virtue through work *Arbeit macht frei*. In 1928 the Weimar government adopted the phrase to promote a policy of large-scale public works. It was common practice in Germany to put wrought-iron inscriptions and *völkisch* symbols on the entry gates to industrial plants and private properties. The incorporation of the words *Arbeit macht frei* on the gates of the Dachau, Terezin, and Auschwitz camps was intended both as a jab at Weimar and as the most tragic irony for those who would lose their lives in slave-labor and extermination camps. The idea of using this slogan came from SS General Theodor Eicke, who was the first commandant of Dachau and inspector general of the entire camp system. Eicke was also responsible for the camp layout itself, which

became the model for all other camps in occupied Europe. Another one of Eicke's conceptions was an identification system for inmates. Implemented in all concentration camps, the system was based on a *Winkel* (inverted triangle) made of variously colored fabrics to distinguish habitual criminals, political enemies, homosexuals, Jehovah's Witnesses, gypsies, and, of course, Jews. This code was initiated shortly after the Nazis opened Dachau in 1933, in a former munitions factory in Bavaria. The camp, initially designed for the "protective custody" of political offenders, soon swelled with the regime's undesirables, who were segregated and then marked for "special treatment."

The six-pointed Star of David was often used to designate Jews in slanderous caricatures at the time, and Stars of David also appeared as anti-Semitic grafitti scrawled on storefronts and office buildings during the early years of Nazism. Yet it was only after the state-sponsored pogrom known as *Kristallnacht* (Night of Broken Glass) in 1938 that Heydrich put forth the official sanction requiring all Jews to wear the yellow star. After Poland was occupied and the ghettos were established, ordinances governing the wearing of the star were strictly enforced. Yellow stars with

DIESER BETRIEB WIRD
VON DER WERKSGEMEINSCHAFT
DER BERUFSORGANISATION
DES GAST-SCHANKGEWERBE
DER N.S.D.A.P. GEFÜHRT.

JUDEN
NICHT ERWÜNSCHT

119

120

the word *Jude* (Jew) in the middle, set in faux-Hebrew lettering, were sold throughout Germany, and Jews were ordered to purchase and wear them. Guidelines also established how and where the stars could be worn, and harsh punishment was meted out if they were creased, folded, or sloppily sewn.

The yellow star, like the concentration-camp badges, served one overarching purpose—immediate, unequivocal identification. Rules were established for how the markings must be worn to ensure that the inmates' status be visible to guards. Charts showing the markings followed a specified format but were often handmade by inmates, who were also called upon to produce other discriminatory signs and placards for the camps. The *Winkel* identification system was not the only standardized design scheme produced in the camps. Prior to the Final Solution, Auschwitz produced *Lagergeld* (camp currency) as well as stationery for prisoners' use. The former were usually small rectangular notes marked with the phrase *Arbeit macht frei* and a colored triangle to indicate the user's provenance. The camp stationery was a self-mailer with a long list of restrictions from the *commandant*, set neatly in blackletter. A bureaucrat-designer who belonged to the Third Reich's graphics department produced the basic templates for these camp materials and then turned them over to skilled inmates to produce.

Ultimately, the Nazis resorted to the most degrading branding technique imaginable: tattooing identification numbers onto inmates' bodies. These were brands in the most literal sense, which could never be erased. The custom began to replace sewn numbers and badges when, in 1941, the Auschwitz complex saw the influx of thousands of Soviet prisoners of war. The tattoo system was created for the Soviets and those deemed "fanatic Communists" were the first to be tattooed on the side of their chests. The letters AU indicating Auschwitz were followed by a number etched into the skin with indelible dye. By 1942, Jews were tattooed as well, and in 1943 almost all of the camp population received this kind of brand, with the exceptions of ethnic Germans, criminal prisoners, and political prisoners.

Primo Levi wrote in his last book, *The Drowned and the Saved*: "The operation was not very painful and lasted no more than a minute, but it was traumatic. Its symbolic meaning was clear to everyone: this is an indelible mark, you will never leave here; this is the mark with which slaves are branded and cattle sent to the slaughter, and that is what you have become. You no longer have a name; this is your new name. The violence of the tattoo was gratuitous, an end in itself, pure offense."[52]

121. **Camp inmates identification system** The Nazis designed coding systems, mostly triangles of different colors, to distinguish and identify the different types of prisoners in concentration camps.

Background: The gate of the Oranienburg concentration camp near Berlin. Welded to the gate is the phrase *Arbeit macht frei* (Work will set you free).

the legacy of nazi design

Parallels between Nazi and commercial identity systems may seem simplistic, but the similarities cannot be ignored. More than in any other totalitarian regime, the iron-fisted management of the Nazi brand came from the top. Hitler and his facilitators understood the value of a wholly integrated system. Despite multiple variations on certain aspects of the overall program, the principal symbol, the swastika, and the familiar visage, the führer, were omnipresent. Sub-brands, like the SS, SA, and HJ, had their own logos, which were modulations of the primary brand. The color palette and the fundamental brand language were by law or decree unalterable. Although the Nazis did not, as many have asserted, develop the archetypical corporate-standards manual, the Promi and the German Labor Front accomplished through caveat the kind of graphic synchronization that major companies spend millions to ensure. The impact of the Nazis' distinct visual language combined with a unique public relations rhetoric comes close to exemplifying how contemporary branding strategies operate.

The American designer Paul Rand once said that a corporate symbol—a logo—is no better or worse than the business it represents. The swastika is not intrinsically evil, but the Nazis put it to evil purposes. And because the power of a political symbol depends on its ability to synthesize an event, ideal, or policy, the Nazi brand is a textbook case of how successful critical mass communication can become. The legacy of the Nazis' branding campaign is its diabolical durability. Even while being horrified by the regime, one must acknowledge the effectiveness of its propaganda. The fact that the swastika elicits such strong emotional responses—that it can still inspire fear and conjure a world of horror—is a sinister testament to the power of the Nazi campaigns.

Opposite:
The ruins of Dresden shown here are typical of the devastation of most German cities. After the surrender, the Allied policy of denazification ordered that all Nazi artifacts be destroyed.
March 1946

the italian fascists

creating the fascist myth

That politics is an art there is no doubt…. At a certain moment the artist creates with inspiration, the politician with decision. Both work with the material and the spirit.

—Benito Mussolini, 1926

inventing the new order

The Nazis' propaganda strategy owed a great debt to Italian Fascism: No figure was more ubiquitous in Italy during the 1920s than Benito Mussolini, who appeared not just in his regalia but also often shirtless for all the world to see. When it came to propagating the heroic image of the Italian leader throughout society, Mussolini had no reservations about being depicted as the virile Roman, and his profile and shaved head became the face of his regime, with a graphic bravado unequaled by any national figure. Reduced to its most elemental form, his image, with protruding chin and searing eye, became a Fascist icon—the quintessential Big Brother.

Mussolini did not aspire to be an artist, as Hitler did, but he was nonetheless a master art dictator of the Fascist style. He did not personally create Fascist designs with pen and pencil, yet he saw to it that signs and symbols representing Fascist Italy were everywhere, and inspirational propaganda spectacles commonplace. He also wrote detailed memoranda to subordinates about the proper display of Fascist party iconography, including specifications about the best display height for optimum viewing. This personal interest had a significant impact on the look of his regime. Mussolini did have literary ambitions, and he even wrote a pulp novel (translated into English as *The Cardinal's Mistress*), an anti-Catholic melodrama serialized in the Socialist magazine *Il popolo* (The people) in 1910. This gave him a modicum of creative credibility, which doubtless fed the hubris that enabled him to impose an overall aesthetic plan on Italy, ranging from retrograde kitsch (Roman classicism) to progressive modernism (Italian Futurism).

The son of a Socialist activist, Mussolini was named after the Mexican reformer Benito Juárez, and he inherited enough of his namesake's bravado to become a leader at a young age in the Italian Socialist party. Becoming editor of the Socialist newspaper *L'avvenire del lavoratore* (The future of the worker) and later *Il popolo*, Mussolini wrote such inflammatory anticlerical and antimonarchist screeds that he was forced to leave Italy. An incendiary ally of the trade unions, he was also arrested and imprisoned a number of times for advocating violence as leverage for negotiations. In 1912 he was appointed editor of *Avanti!* (Forward!), the official newspaper of the Socialist party. In this role Mussolini was vociferously antinationalist and antimilitaristic; he was initially strongly opposed to Italy's involvement in World War I, but soon changed his mind and began writing articles in favor of intervention. He resigned from the paper and was expelled from the Socialist party. In 1914 he formed the militant Milan-based Fasci d'Azione Rivoluzionaria (Revolutionary Action League) and founded a new radical newspaper, *Il popolo d'Italia* (The people of Italy), ostensibly serving as its editor and art director until its demise in 1943.

122. *Vincere* (To win)
This illustration by Walter Roveroni for the cover of *L'industria della stampa* cleverly fashions Mussolini's profile out of stacked helmets. 1941

123. *Fiera del Levante* (Fair of the East)
This periodical cover by Piquillo promoted Bari's annual trade fair, the Fiera del Levante. 1934

Background:
Mussolini addressing a crowd from a balcony in Pistoia. 26 May 1930

Previous spread:
Fascist rally in Rome. Date unknown

122

123

L'INDUSTRIA DELLA STAMPA

VINCERE

W IL DUCE

MARZO-APRILE 1941-XIX - N. 3-4

FIERA DEL LEVANTE BARI

PERIODICO DI PROPAGANDA

Anno IV · N. 1   GENNAIO - APRILE 1934-XII

In 1915 Mussolini was drafted into the Italian army, where he served until 1917. During that time he maintained a personal diary (a parallel to Hitler's *Mein Kampf*, which was written almost ten years later), in which he charted his trajectory toward becoming the supreme "Duce" (*dux* in Latin— duke, or leader) of an antibourgeois revolutionary state composed of ideological combatants and conformist followers. In this diary-cum-blueprint, Mussolini outlined an ideology wedded to an aesthetic plan that underscored the graphic identity of his "revolution."

Soon after the war, in 1919, Mussolini restructured the Milan *fascio* into the Fasci Italiani di Combattimento (Italian Fighting League). The word *fascio* (fasces) was a common term in Italy at the time for factional political groups, left or right, and was sometimes also used for nonpolitical organizations. It is a testament to the effectiveness of Mussolini's branding campaign that it eventually became associated exclusively with his ultranationalist, militaristic regime, and is now commonly used to characterize movements showing traits similar to the Italian dictatorship. The *fascio*'s members, known as *fascisti* (Fascists), were organized into armed paramilitary squads, identifiable by one consistent piece of apparel, the *camicia nera* (black shirt; other uniform accoutrements were too expensive at that time). The *fascisti*, who were soon referred to simply as Blackshirts, exerted a significant stylistic influence on politics and fashion, bringing the two together in an unprecedented way. But Mussolini was not the innovator here; the idea of identification by shirt color had been introduced in Italy during the Risorgimento, the nineteenth-century Italian nationalist movement, when Giuseppe Garibaldi's *camicie rosse* (Redshirts) fought to end foreign occupation and unify the Italian nation. Mussolini's Blackshirts were the first paramilitary group to emulate Garibaldi's troops in this respect, but

124. *Benito Mussolini, capo del governo–duce del fascismo* (head of the government, leader of Fascism)
One of hundreds of souvenir postcards sold at the many rallies and pageants promoting the Fascist regime. c. 1935

125. *Il popolo d'Italia* (The people of Italy)
This poster advertises the newspaper founded by Mussolini and edited by his brother Arnaldo. The text proclaims, "Read it all! Read it, everyone!" c. 1935

126. Blackshirts
Mussolini with Blackshirts in Rome. 1922

between the wars color-coded shirts became a common method of identification for various international Fascist and nationalist movements in Great Britain, France, Austria, Eastern Europe, and even the United States.

In the fall of 1921 Mussolini was elected to parliament, and he organized scattered groups of like-minded extremists into the Partito Nazionale Fascista (PNF; National Fascist Party). It took as its emblem the *fascio littorio* (lictorian fasces), a bundle of rods tied around an ax, symbolizing strength and authority, that had been ceremoniously carried by "lictors," or magistrate attendants, in the Roman Republic. This *fascio* provided both the name and the metaphor for the party, symbolizing the notion of strength in unity—a single stick is easily broken, but a bundle is unbreakable. As his popularity grew, Mussolini began to establish a new narrative designed to underscore his quest for power. In a speech delivered in Naples on 24 October 1922, he proclaimed: "We have created our myth. The myth is a faith, it is passion. It is not

necessary that it shall be a reality. It is a reality by the fact that it is a good, a hope, a faith, that it is courage. Our myth is the Nation, our myth is the greatness of the Nation! And to this myth, to this grandeur, which we wish to translate into a complete reality, we subordinate all the rest."[1]

On 27 October 1922, the cornerstone of the Fascist branding myth was laid when Mussolini sent his *squadristi* (squads) to march on Rome, a move that forced King Vittorio Emanuele III to invite the minority party to form Italy's new government, with Mussolini as prime minister. Mussolini touted the March on Rome as a coup, but in fact the transfer of power was within the laws of the constitution, though it was achieved through intimidation. It did propel Mussolini to a new position of power; he immediately began instituting laws that eroded the democratic institutions, and he used his Fascist militias to silence the opposition. Three years later, on the day Mussolini declared himself dictator, he announced, "Today in Italy is not the time for history.... It is the time for

127. *La pace con onore e con giustizia e la pace romana* (Peace with honor and justice is Roman peace)
Il Duce's distinctive silhouette became the unmistakable logo for the Fascist regime.
1936

128. *Il Duce alle gerarchie di Roma* (Il Duce and the hierarchy of Rome)
Mussolini is montaged against the standards of the old Roman Empire, suggesting that he is the emperor of the New Rome.
1941

129. *Credere* (Believe)
Mussolini's catchword is superimposed on his monogram, *M.*
1934

130. *DUX* (Leader)
This image makes Mussolini almost Caesar-like, a quality reinforced by the use of the Latin Dux, written in Roman style (DVX).
Date unknown

131. *MVSN Anno XVII* (MVSN year 17)
Cover for the annual calendar of the Milizia Volontaria per la Sicurezza Nazionale (MVSN; Voluntary Militia for National Security), illustrated by Giuseppe "Pippi" Starace with a typically heroic portrait of Mussolini.
1939

Background:
Boys posing in the small town of Capalbio, where a stenciled portrait of Mussolini sits above one of his favorite mottos: "Believe, obey, fight."
Date unkown

myths…. Only the myth can give strength and energy to a people about to hammer out its own destiny."[2]

Myths of a new empire, of a New Man—the restoration *and* the innovation of a great state—were planted in the fertile minds of Italian citizens. These myths were instilled primarily through extensive graphic campaigns featuring a distinctive Fascist style that purported to replace staid bourgeois designs with revolutionary symbols and icons. Mussolini understood that for Fascism to permeate society, every facet of Italian life needed to be revamped. Aided by his slavishly devoted party vice secretary, Achille Starace (who served from 1931 to 1939), he enacted a nationwide Reforma delle Abitudini (Reform of customs), an imposed overhaul of daily life and habits—the Italian cognate of the Nazis' *Gleichschaltung*. The Roman calendar was changed so that 1922 (when the Fascists assumed power) became Anno I; the linguistic system was altered so that the formal forms of address, *lei* and *loro*, were officially abolished and replaced by the informal, egalitarian second-person singular *tu* and plural *voi*; all dialects were outlawed as remnants of inglorious former foreign occupations; and the handshake was eliminated in favor of the straight-armed Roman salute. Above all, the national symbols of Italy, including the flag, were exchanged for new Fascist emblems. Fascist style, initially managed through the Ministero della Pubblica Istruzione (Ministry of Public Instruction), was enforced in all media, from commercial advertising to architecture. Starting in the early 1920s, even quotidian commercial products were given new names with Fascist overtones: the Agip brand of gasoline was redubbed Littoria, and a passenger train was given the name Littorina (both after the lictors of ancient Rome).

The omnipresent three-quarter visage of Il Duce was posted all over Italy, rendered in painting,

129

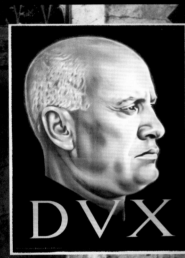

130

131

132. Salute
Bicyclists saluting
Mussolini with letters
spelling out his name
pinned to their shirts.
November 1923

133. Mussolini
Children on the beach
at the seaside resort
of Anzio spell out
Mussolini in giant
living letters.
3 September 1937

134. *SI SI SI* (yes yes yes)
An enormous effigy
of Mussolini looks
down from a banner
facing the Palazzo
Braschi in Rome.
1934

133

stone, and high-contrast black-and-white stencils on buildings and bridges. It was required that "DUCE" be spelled out in Roman capitals whenever the word appeared in print. Mussolini's campaign had a big influence on Hitler, who was already beginning to craft his National Socialist image in Germany and who admired the pomp and circumstance that Il Duce brought to politics. In addition to the straight-armed salute, Hitler borrowed Roman symbols and visual trappings. (Hitler's propaganda ministry ultimately became even more efficient than the Fascists in flooding the nation with iconography.)

Il Duce was also adept at coining and then ceaselessly repeating phrases and mottos that, like incessant advertising jingles, infiltrated the mass subconscious. Mussolini had his quotations stenciled on countless buildings and walls throughout Italy. The most common was *"Mussolini ha sempre ragione"* (Mussolini is always right), but there were many others, including "Fascism is a house of glass into which everyone can look"; "A book and a rifle make a perfect Fascist"; "Inactivity is death"; "A plow makes the furrow but the sword will defend it"; "Let us have a dagger between our teeth, a bomb in our hands, and

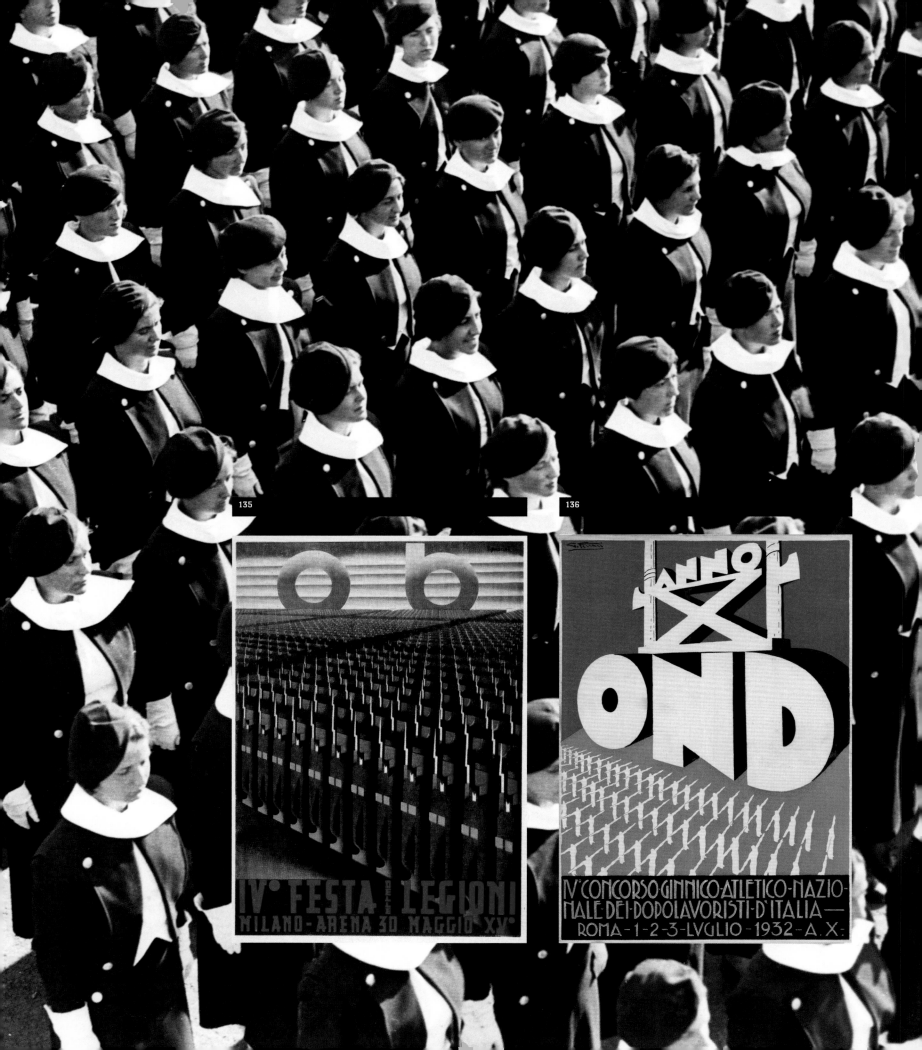

135

136

IV° FESTA DELLE LEGIONI
MILANO · ARENA 30 MAGGIO · XV·

L'ANNO X
OND
IV° CONCORSO · GINNICO · ATLETICO · NAZIO-
NALE · DEI · DOPOLAVORISTI · D'ITALIA —
ROMA · 1 · 2 · 3 · LVGLIO · 1932 · A · X ·

135. *IV Festa delle legioni*
(Fourth festival of legions)
Poster designed by
Franco Signorini for a
gathering of the Fascist
youth organization
Opera Balilla in Milan.
1937

136. *Anno X OND*
(Year 10 OND)
Poster designed by
G. Pessani for the Opera
Nazionale Dopolavoro,
the Fascist leisure and
recreational organi-
zation, in celebration of
the tenth anniversary
of the Fascist revolution.
The bold shadowed
lettering was typical
of Fascist typography
and a symbol of
state power over the
individual.
1932

137. *DUX* (Leader)
Il Duce or Dux (the
Roman spelling) were
used as frequently as
Mussolini's own
name. This postcard
illustrated by Ernesto
Michahelles Thayaht
was designed to
celebrate the military
and physical training
mandated under
Il Duce's rule.
1929

Background:
Parade of the Giovani
Italiane (Young Italians),
a fascist organization
for young women.
c. 1935

an infinite scorn in our hearts"; and the ubiquitous "Believe, obey, fight"—often affixed with Mussolini's signature or a calligraphed *M*.

A central flaw in Mussolini's branding strategy was that, despite all the bombastic rhetoric and military adventurism—not to mention the Fascists' famous ability to make the Italian trains run on time— Mussolinian mythology focused on the appearance, not the substance, of Fascism. When Fascism first began as a movement, its policies were rather vague. The image-savvy Mussolini devoted more time to publicity than to policy. Grandiosity was its own reward: A glossy veneer gave the illusion of authority— and it was an illusion that Mussolini himself believed. So efficiently was Fascism branded, through symbolic and concrete manifestations—from uniforms to buildings, from the Roman salute to the *passo romano*, or Italian goose step—that Mussolini himself became infatuated with the Fascist myth. His son-in-law, Count Galeazzo Ciano, who briefly served as the Fascist minister of press and propaganda before becoming

foreign minister, recognized this when he observed that during military parades, "[Mussolini] spends hours at the window of his office hidden behind the blue curtains, spying the movements of his troops.... He more and more believes that form ... determines substance."[3] He deluded himself into confusing Fascist style with content—and at the same time fooled admirers of his regime elsewhere in the world (early editorials in the *New York Times* praised him).

Mussolini constructed Fascism from a haphazard patchwork of sociopolitical ideas he had surveyed as a young man. Political historian William Ebenstein explains: "From Aristotle [Fascism] derived the view of the inborn inequality of men together with the mon- archical theory of the state; from Plato the concept of the privileged class which holds a monopoly of political power, and which can be trained for its tasks through an elaborate system of artistic, scientific and civic education. From Machiavelli it inherits the legacy of political realism, the dissociation of politics from ethics and morality, the concept of the reason of the state as

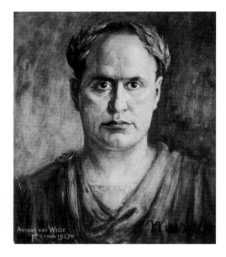

a guiding criterion in the pursuit of the social good."[4] Fascism adhered to tenets that were hostile to the ideas of natural law and popular sovereignty. Conservative (and racialist) German theorist Heinrich Gotthard von Treitschke made a deep impression upon the Fascist conception of the state and its place in the international community. The Fascists also distorted Georg Wilhelm Friedrich Hegel's idea of the corporate state.

    "The state, as Fascism conceives it and carries it out, is a spiritual and moral fact, since it makes the political, juridical and economic organization of the nation concrete," wrote Mussolini. "In the Fascist concept the people is the State and the State is the people."[5] In reality, Fascism was emphatically ruled by a minority elite, not by "the people": Fascists believed that the body existed for the benefit of the brain, the individual for the benefit of the general good.

    In such thinking lies the essence of totalitarianism, which in Mussolini's view was the highest virtue a state and leader could achieve. Fascism distilled this hodgepodge of sociopolitical theories into a simple message firmly impressed on the popular consciousness through graphic images that reduced individuals to the pattern in a totalitarian fabric. Posters showing rows of uniformly regimented Fascist youth and militia were as common as the endless parades in which they marched, in lockstep, for the world to see. Fascist visuals underscored the notion that the people were servants of the state, and the state was Il Duce.

symbolizing the new man

Mussolini's aim was to construct a new order built upon a unifying foundation—a kind of lay religion with a newly fabricated liturgy. In this endeavor to create a Fascist visual identity, Mussolini was greatly influenced by the nationalist poet Gabriele d'Annunzio. In 1919, d'Annunzio invaded the port city of Fiume (now Rijeka, in Croatia) in defiance of the Versailles Treaty, which proposed to incorporate Fiume into the new Yugoslavia. D'Annunzio created an elitist government of which he became the self-proclaimed dictator. During his one-year tenure, d'Annunzio developed a litany of signs and symbols, as well as a constitution that established Fiume as the first "corporate state." He employed tactics of stagecraft and ritual, instituted the Roman salute, and dressed his soldiers in black shirts. Even though d'Annunzio's small-scale revolution did not translate onto the national stage, it did provide a model for Mussolini, who adapted many of the poet's political ideas and visual trappings.

    Mussolini invented himself as inextricably intertwined with the party, and with the state, to the extent that he himself became a national symbol. His devoted right-hand man, Achille Starace, helped craft the cult of Il Duce. An early member of the party, Starace had participated in the March on Rome in 1922. He held many key positions, including general of the Milizia Volontaria per la Sicurezza Nazionale

(MVSN; Voluntary Militia for National Security); member of the Italian Chamber of Deputies; and ultimately, in 1931, secretary of the Fascist party. The devoted factotum who worked to propagate Il Duce's image through pageants and parades, he built four cults based on the myth of Mussolini's power: the cults of hero worship, violence, war, and Romanism. Each cultist sensibility was made concrete in the art and design produced for the state. Mussolini was the sole hero, often portrayed as the new Caesar. His legions, from youth organizations to militia, were depicted in black uniforms, poised for action, with batons and guns at the ready, protectors of the Fascist flame.

Mussolini's vision of the new Italian state was young and masculine, strong and virile. Overtly sexist, he considered women to be the weaker sex. He referred to the masses as female, implying that they were moody and irrational and hence incapable of commanding themselves, and he used this to justify the concept of a strongman as head of state. This prompted him to exaggerate his masculine image. Mussolini appeared on countless book and magazine covers in the manner of a movie star, and liberal use was made of the air-brush. A great number of images show him riding on horseback or flying an airplane; such depictions played a crucial part in his wide perception as a sex symbol and as the personification of masculinity. And for the dictator's women followers, the party issued an annual calendar that featured recipes as well as photographs of a gallant Il Duce and one of his quotations for each month of the year. He further publicized his virility by placing myriad massive busts and figures of himself throughout Italy, some of them unabashedly phallic. Directly related to this phallic symbolism was a barrage of images that portrayed faceless heroic Fascists as paradigms of Italian manhood. But Mussolini also honed a paternalistic image, purporting to protect his people through his strong-armed embrace— firm yet nurturing—as long as they complied with the will of the state.

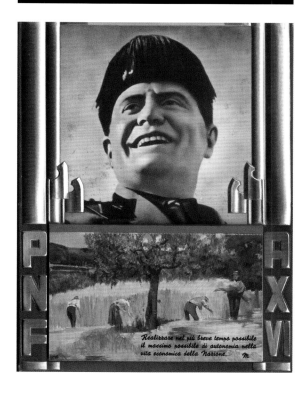

138. Il Duce as model
Mussolini posing for American sculptor Jo Davidson. Many such busts were placed in official buildings and offices.
1927

139. Il Duce as Caesar
Mussolini is depicted as Julius Caesar in this portrait by Antoon Van Welie, painter of popes, nobility, and society figures.
1927

140. Il Duce on horseback
This portrait titled "The eagles," by Giuseppe Palanti, is one of many with Mussolini on horseback in his regalia.
Date unknown

141. Il Duce as aviator
This calendar published by the Italian Insurance Institute portrays Mussolini as a pilot, yet another depiction of Il Duce's masculinity.
1928

142. P[artito] N[azionale] F[ascista] A[nno] XVI (National Fascist Party year 16)
Calendars such as this one were issued every year by the Fascist Party.
1938

Equally iconic in the Italian Fascist visual scheme were representations of violence: The idea of force was indispensable to the overall brand narrative. "It is blood which gives movement to the wheel of history," proclaimed Mussolini.[6] Violence was celebrated in early Fascist song titles such as "A colpi di pugnale la giustizia si fara" (Justice will be carried out with dagger thrusts) and "Ad uno ad uno li ammazzarem" (We will kill them one by one). The *manganello* (truncheon or cudgel), the primary weapon of the Fascist *squadristi*, was a vivid symbol of their mission. It had been used as a weapon during the Risorgimento, but under Il Duce it was so integral to the notion of power that a variety of manufacturers put their versions of the *manganello* on the retail market. Posters and magazine covers depicted heroic—and glamorous—Blackshirts proudly carrying cudgels as part of their uniform gear; even youth groups were issued *manganelli* as standard equipment. These truncheons were not merely symbolic; a standing order was issued to party members to bash skulls to enforce Fascist ideas. Attacks against Communists and Social Democrats were so common that the newspapers stopped bothering to report them. At a 1923 celebration marking the first anniversary of the March on Rome, Mussolini said, "The Revolution was made with clubs…thanks to the heroism of the Blackshirts; now it is to be defended and consolidated with arms and guns."[7] He branded his *squadristi* with the motto "Me ne frego" (I don't give a damn), which was written on the bandages covering their wounds. This stoic stance was part of what Il Duce called "a new style of Italian life."

War, according to Mussolini, was a Fascist ritual, and a natural impulse: "War is to man what child-rearing is to a woman."[8] War was promoted as the cleansing of the old and stagnant elements of society, and violence as the engine of renewal. Mussolini praised war for its dynamism: "Fascism…does not believe in the possibility of the utility of perpetual

143. Il Duce statue
This colossal statue of Mussolini dominated the Vanguardisti (Fascist Youth) training camp outside Rome, where teenagers prepared to become Fascist soldiers. 1934

144. *Attività politica* (Political activity)
A gun-toting Mussolini appears in this hand-book published by the Gruppi Universitari Fascisti (GUF; University Fascist Group). Il Duce is montaged onto a bust sculpted in 1926 by Adolfo Wildt. 1929

Background:
After Haile Selassie's defeat, the Fascist victors sculpted this enormous head of Mussolini in the Ethiopian landscape. 1936

ATTIVITÀ
POLITICA

peace," he wrote. "It therefore rejects that pacifism which hides a renunciation of struggle and a cowardice in the face of sacrifice. Only war brings all human energies to their maximum tension and impresses a seal of nobility on peoples who have the courage to meet it."[9] Mussolini used this rhetoric of war to justify his expansionist aspirations. Italy's loss of its Eritrean colony in 1896 had been felt as a humiliating national defeat, and when Mussolini sought to invade and reclaim the colony in 1935, the Italian people were enthusiastic, seeing this as fulfilling Mussolini's promise to rebuild the Roman Empire. Propaganda, often aimed at schoolchildren in textbooks and on the covers of *quaderni* (assignment booklets), portrayed Ethiopians as savages and Italian soldiers as heroes of civilization. Though the campaign was a disaster, and the Italians committed atrocities in Ethiopia, the war coincided with the regime's highest levels of popularity.

dreaming of the new rome

"Rome is our departure and reference point: it is our symbol or, if you wish, our Myth. We dream of Roman Italy, i.e. wise and strong, disciplined and imperial."[10] Though Fascist style evolved through various iterations and famously embraced some aspects of Futurism, the imperial Roman symbols—eagles, standards, daggers, and, of course, the *fascio*—were the foundation of Fascist aesthetics.

Although Mussolini appropriated both the term and the symbol, the *fascio* had a history before its co-option by the Fascists. Introduced by French revolutionaries as a symbol of republicanism, it was used by fighters of the Italian Risorgimento. (To this day, two *fasci* hang in the American Congress and frame the U.S. president during the yearly State of the Union address.)

The *fascio* initially appeared in two designs, one that showed the ax head to the side of the rods (the "Roman" version), the other with the ax atop them in the center. Mussolini charged an eminent archaeologist with the task of researching the original details

145. *Me ne frego*
(**I don't give a damn**)
This postcard com-
memorates the street
fights of the early days
of Fascism from the
movement's creation
in 1919 to the takeover
of power in 1922.
1934

146. *Presente alle
bandiere* (**Salute the flag**)
The Roman dagger
was another symbol
of Fascist power. This
poster by Antonio
Rigorini shows all the
trappings of the state,
and commands that the
dagger be held high.
c. 1944

147. Piazza del Duomo
Fascist rally in the
square in front of Milan's
historic cathedral.
Date unknown

MINISTERO EDVCAZIONE NAZIONALE

OP. NAZ. "BALILLA"

148. Report card
Report cards such as
this one, designed by
Cesare Gobbo, were
issued to all members
of the Opera Nazionale
Balilla.
1930

149. Fascist labor
The marriage of
industry and politics
was a key element
of Fascism, symbolized
by this heroic depiction
of labor and militia.
1924

150. Fascist agriculture
The Fascists established
various projects
to boost the economy.
This poster for the
Confederazione Fascista
dei Lavoratori dell'
Agricoltura (Fascist
Confederation of
Agricultural Workers)
combines *fasci* and
spades as symbols
of Italy's agricultural
progress.
1935

of the design and its historical transformations; he wanted to be certain the symbol was being correctly used. After the decree of 12 December 1926 made the *fascio* an emblem of the state, the Roman version prevailed. The official decree also ordered that the *fascio littorio* either sit beside or replace the old Italian emblems wherever they appeared. The sign no longer represented simply the Fascist party; it had become the symbol of the new national regime.

 Fasci became ubiquitous throughout Italy and appeared on most official and many unofficial objects. Monumental *fascio* sculptures were erected in the streets and adorned the facades of buildings.[11] The *fascio* badge became an obligatory accessory to civilian clothes (the sale of unauthorized badges was forbidden), and propaganda films depicted reenactments of the Roman lictors in procession, carrying the symbolic *fascio*. Whereas in Germany unsanctioned

commercial applications of the swastika were illegal, the use of the *fascio* in Italy was encouraged in countless commercial advertisements, package designs, and product displays. In this way Mussolini ensured that this key Fascist symbol—the image that tied the nation together as a conformist whole—was fully integrated into Italian life. Fascism was promoted as a way of life, and the party iconography, particularly the *fascio*, was omnipresent on posters and advertisements for coffee, banks, and travel services, among other things. Italy's most skilled graphic designers—among them Federico Seneca, Erberto Carboni, and Oscar Signorini—transformed everyday products into personifications of the Fascist spirit through advertising that wed the mundane with the alleged virtues of the New Order. The challenge most commonly faced by artists and designers was how to include the *fascio* in a work of art or design;

they devised various clever ways to stylize the emblem,
amplifying its symbolic strength. Finding the *fascio*
in an image became something of a national pastime.

Unlike the swastika, the *fascio* was designed
in various stylistic iterations, from the classical to
the ultramodern. Strict design guidelines were not
imposed, so interpretations were often the prerogative
of the individual artist or designer. Classical versions
were very detailed—revealing every stick tied with
a rope or leather binding around the ax blade—while
modernist renditions, influenced by the more streamlined Futurist styles, were flat silhouettes of a more
reductive form. Often the *fascio* was so abstractly
minimalist (the sticks and ax head fused into a single
mass) that it was nearly unrecognizable.

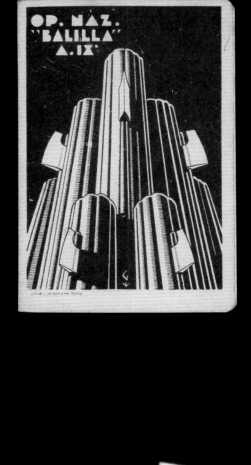

fascist style

fascist carnival aesthetics

Fascist aesthetics seem curiously carnivalesque in comparison with the rigid Nazi style. The Nazis undoubtedly produced the twentieth century's most effective totalitarian propaganda campaign, based on a strict graphic identity program. Fascist designers, on the other hand, created a more eclectic visual language, and the trend toward bombastic monumentalism, so apparent in other totalitarian regimes, was somewhat less pronounced in Italy, at least at first. While Fascist style also extolled the heroic—in graphics, artworks, and monuments— it was much less in evidence in Italy than in Germany. But even though the Fascist campaign to ensnare the masses through an overarching aesthetic was not rigidly homogeneous, it was decidedly influential. The swastika proved to be a more hypnotic symbol than the *fascio*, but the critical mass of icons, images, and accoutrements that constituted the Fascist style was just as omnipresent.

Unlike in Germany, where commercial artists were required to belong to official trade chambers, Italian graphic artists did not have to be registered, and they were not strictly monitored unless they chose to join the Fascist party. Their work simply had to show that they shared Fascist ideals. From the beginning, Mussolini received enthusiastic support from the vanguard of modern Italian art: the Futurists. Although Futurism's radical manifestos were doubtless repellent to many old-guard Fascists, Futurism's visual bravado served the Fascist message well, signaling a change in spirit as well as in aesthetics. Futurism had originated a decade before Mussolini launched the Fascist movement; impressed by the promise of a revolutionary party, its founder, Filippo Tommaso Marinetti, threw Futurism's support behind Il Duce. His *Futurist Manifesto* of 1909 had been a call to battle: "United we must attack!... There can be no nostalgia! No pessimism!... Forward! Faster! Farther! Higher!" Futurism espoused the idea of a permanent artistic and political revolution. Traditionalism was rejected in favor of "the new religion of speed." The Futurists mythologized machines—first the automobile and later the airplane—as totems of the modern spirit. Speed was a welcome disruptive force, a weapon to agitate and propel society into the future. Boisterous publicity campaigns promoted Futurist events that were part theater, part rally, and part rabble-rousing. The movement's influence was indisputable (and not only on Fascist culture—Futurism had a powerful impact on modern art in general).

Futurist ideas were first expressed through free-verse orchestrations of sound and image that were made manifest in new, kinetic typographies. "The typographic revolution was initiated by me," wrote Marinetti, "and directed especially against the so-called typographic harmony of the page."[12]

155. *O Roma o morte* **(Rome or death)**
Once the war was under way, posters became more aggressive. Although this is not as heroically representational as many others, it attempts to trigger atavistic and patriotic feelings. c. 1943

156. *La strade statali d'Italia* **(Italian state highways)**
The cover of this road map, illustrated by C.V. Testi, uses airbrushing to project Roman symbols in a contemporary manner. 1934

Background:
Mussolini on horseback greets Blackshirts in the Colosseum. 1930

155

156

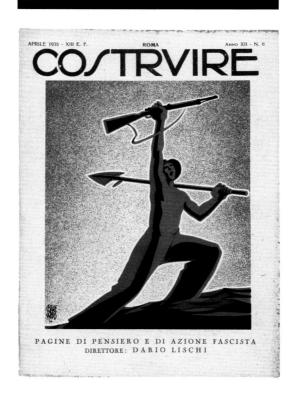

157. *Assistenza fascista*
(**Fascist assistance**)
The cover of this
magazine devoted to
Fascist social welfare
employs Moderne
lettering for its logo.
The quotation by
Mussolini about the
difference between
philanthropy and
assistance is typeset to
look like an inscription
on a column.
1941

158. *Almanacco fascista*
del popolo d'Italia
(**Fascist almanac of the**
people of Italy)
Cover of the almanac of
Mussolini's newspaper
with an impressionistic
portrayal of the *fascio*
and cannon, with hand-
lettered typography by
Mario Sironi.
1936

159–60. *Costruire* (**Build**)
These magazine covers
were illustrated by
Cesare Gobbo, who
designed many Fascist
party periodicals.
1935

161. *Elementi di coltura fascista* (Elements of Fascist culture)
The cover of this text-book for members of the Balilla organization is illustrated in a straightforward realism, in contrast to many more stylized images. c. 1936

162. MVSN handbook
This guide for the paramilitary Fascist militia is designed using a Moderne sans serif lettering style frequently seen on posters and commercial advertisements. 1933

163. *La difesa della stirpe* (Defense of origin)
This magazine cover uses a typeface found in some Futurist periodicals. 1938

Rather than one or two typographic variations per page, Marinetti used as many as twenty different fonts of various weights, each with its own significance; italic stood for motion, and boldface for violence. He also rejected traditional syntax: He eliminated adjectives and adverbs and made liberal use of onomatopoeia. Futurist aesthetics were soon applied to all possible media, from painting and sculpture to furniture and radios. The intent was to create a visual vocabulary suggestive of the "whirling world of steel, pride, fever, and speed."[13]

Fortunato Depero—a Futurist painter, fashion designer, and advertising artist who also referred to himself as a critic, architect, sculptor, musician, mathematician, physicist, chemist, lecturer, soldier, crazy man, and free complex genius—also played an important role in linking Fascism with Futurist aesthetics. His dazzling modern graphic vocabulary prefigures late-twentieth-century postmodern and New Wave eclecticism. With Giacomo Ballà, Depero wrote in *Ricostruzione futurista dell'universo* (1915; Futurist reconstruction of the universe), "We Futurists…want to create this total fusion in order to reconstruct the universe, cheering it up… according to the whim of our inspiration."[14] Depero channeled Futurism's raw expression into an alluring visual language and typography, adding elements

of Cubism, Expressionism, and primitivism to a distinctive conceptual vocabulary. His speed-inspired block lettering—often with sharp points and angles to suggest bolts of lightning—helped define the graphic sensibility of the 1930s. He was by far the most inventive graphic designer of the era in Italy, and his recurring references to the *fascio* and other symbols of Fascism helped to propagate the regime's fabricated aura of progressiveness.

Renato Bertelli's *Profilo continuo del Duce* (Continuous profile of Il Duce) from 1933 is a monument to the fusion of Futurism and Fascism. The wood sculpture of Mussolini's face gives the illusion of perpetual spinning motion. It is a tip of the hat to Janus, the double-faced Roman god of beginnings and endings, who was worshipped at times of transitions—the change of seasons, the start of a new year—and also represented such interdependent opposites as war and peace. The sculpture exemplifies Futurism's play with opposites and its skill at investing static art with the illusion of speed.

Futurism, however, was not to become the official Fascist style. Insofar as there was an official style, by the early 1930s it had evolved into a relatively lifeless monumental-rhetorical academicism. Much to Marinetti's disappointment, Mussolini's pronouncements on art and architecture were

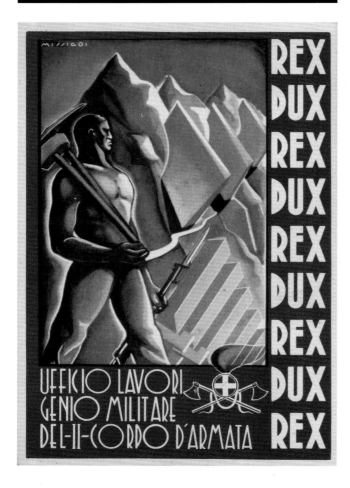

inconsistent, and eventually, as real politics took precedence, he abandoned Futurist ideals. Mussolini's tastes ran more toward the monumental than the experimental. He also seemed to prefer the Novecento style, which originated in 1926 and was characterized by a stripped-down neoclassicism inspired by the geometric decorative tendencies found in Art Deco.

Art Moderne, the Fascist variant of Art Deco, was another nod to "young" aesthetics and a powerful tool for Fascist artists, who made use of the style to signal youth and suggest the power of the regime. Art Moderne smoothed away the cracks in Roman antiquities and brought these artifacts of Italy's glorious past up to date. Airbrushed surfaces symbolized the machine-age progress that Mussolini sought. The illustrator known as Tato (Guglielmo Sansoni) introduced a polemical style in which

a streamlined variant of Cubism was employed to dynamically represent youthful Fascist militia.

Compared to the *völkisch* revival in Germany, there was far less interest in folk culture in Italy (although there was a brand of Fascist provincialism called Strapaese—rural or "native land" style), and no attempt was made to revive pagan rituals. The Fascists drew from their "roots" in a different way, with Romanism as a means to restore Italy's imperial Roman glories—the antithesis of a folk culture. Mussolini did not try to revive a musty old era, but made use of it to build a new aesthetic. Unlike in Germany, where the avant-garde was defamed in the *Entartete Kunst* (Degenerate art) exhibitions and then brutally eliminated, the divergence between "free" art and state art did not seem to faze Mussolini. In Fascist Italy, modern art was never the pariah it became in Nazi Germany. While the argument raged

164. *Rex Dux*
(King Leader)
Fascist romantic realism
or Heroic Realism, here
exemplified by Missigoi,
was typical of many
posters that conflated
the Fascist New Man and
the regal reign of Il Duce.
c. 1935

165. *Mostra della*
rivoluzione fascista
(Exhibition of the
Fascist revolution)
This poster, designed
by C.V. Testi, celebra-
ting the eleventh
anniversary of the
Fascist revolution,
represents three kinds
of Fascist fighters
(distinguished by their
headwear), each posed
much like Il Duce.
1933

166. *Profilo continuo*
del Duce **(Continuous**
profile of Il Duce)
This Futurist bronzed
terra-cotta sculpture,
by Renato Bertelli,
was later reproduced
in multiples, with
Mussolini's approval.
1933

ROMA - CHICAGO -
NEW YORK - ROMA

CROCIERA AEREA
DEL DECENNALE 1933 - XI

167. *Crociera aerea del decennale* (Air cruise of the decade)
This poster, designed by Marcello Dudovich, features planes flying in formation in the shape of a *fascio*.
1933

168. *I focolari proteggi dall'odio nemico! Arruolatevi nei reparti contraerei* (Protect your homes from enemy hatred! Enlist in anti-aircraft units)
Graphic styles became more turgidly heroic when the virtues of warfare had to be sold to the populace.
c. 1940

169. *Lavorare e combattere per la patria, per la vittoria* (Work and fight for the homeland, for victory)
As the war progressed, Fascist style veered toward Heroic Realism.
1944

between classicists and modernists over what art was best suited to evoke the Fascist spirit, both cohabitated in comparative harmony, at least at the outset of the regime.

fascist typography

Novel typefaces, some influenced by Futurism, were used to promote Fascism. Expressive type was intended to transform Mussolini's slogans into forceful battle cries. Central-axis page composition was replaced by a more dynamic aesthetic that wed Futurism to Art Deco—controlled anarchy to decorative mannerism. Typefaces with sharp edges and contoured right angles expressing velocity and stencil-based letterforms, like Braggadocio, replaced "old-fashioned" classic Roman alphabets, especially in propaganda aimed at the young. Often these newly designed letters

were set in tight blocks, reminiscent of monumental stone inscriptions (and formations of Roman soldiers), combining a contemporary look with an aura of classical virtue.

When the Fascists changed the Italian linguistic system, the shift was supported by a radical typographic restyling that rejected "humanist" serifs for demonstrative Gothics or sans serifs.

CONFEDERAZIONE NAZIONALE DEI SINDACATI FASCISTI DELL'INDUSTRIA

Stab. A. MARZI Roma

170. *Confederazione Nazionale dei Sindacati Fascisti dell'Industria* (National Confederation of Fascist Industrial Unions)
This identity card for an industrial workers' union creates an analogy between the chimneys of Italian factories and the *fascio.*
1932

171. *III Raduno Naz[ionale] Artiglieri* (Third National Artillery rally)
This stylized rendering by F. Walter projects a more playful aesthetic than conventional military posters.
1934

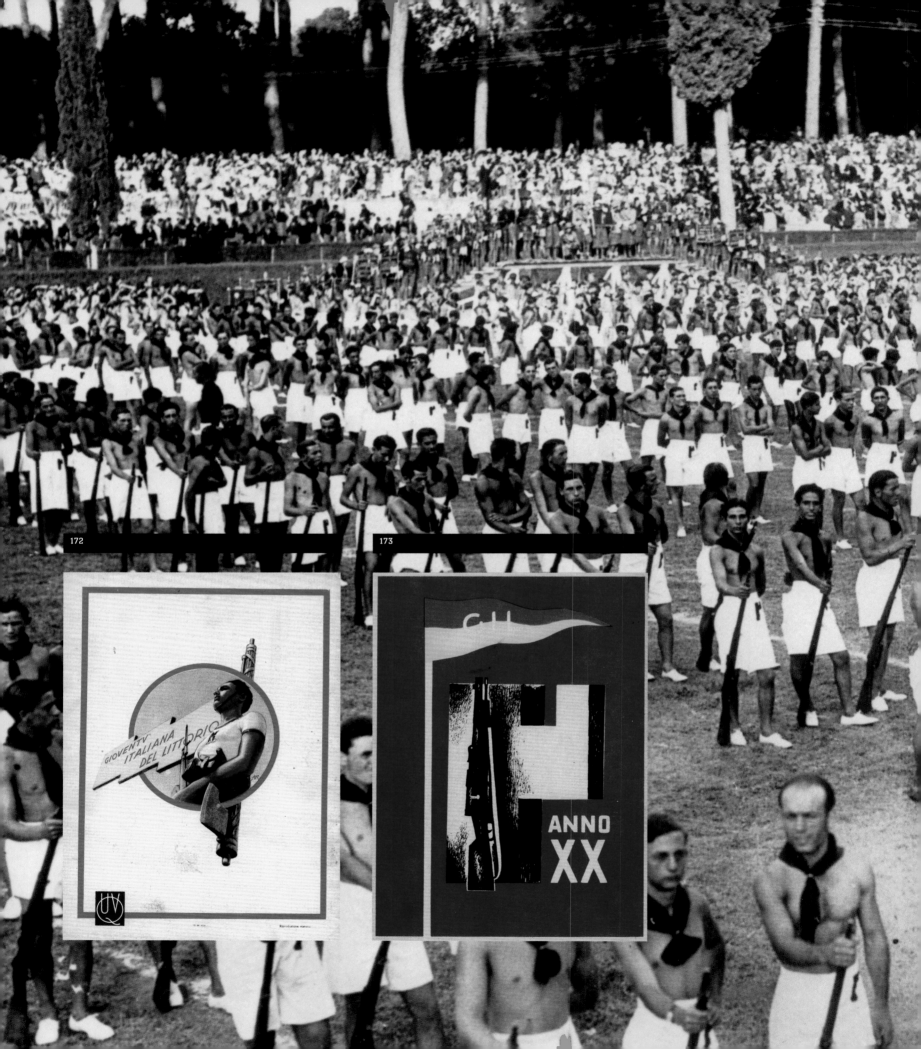

172

173

promoting empire

harnessing fascist youth

Fascism proclaimed youth the most valuable asset of the state. The shock troops of Fascism were originally gangs of unbridled youths storming through Italy wearing black shirts and jackboots, carrying death's-head flags, and wielding batons against the declared enemy: social decay and cultural elitism. Mussolini instituted youth organizations that included eight- to twenty-one-year-olds. The first such group was the Avanguardia Studentesca dei Fasci Italiani di Combattimento (Italian Fascist Fighting Student Front), founded in 1920 under the control of the Milan *fascio*. It began publishing a magazine titled *Giovinezza* (Youth). In 1921 the group became the Avanguardia Giovanile Fascista (Fascist Youth Front, also known as the Vanguardisti) for boys from fifteen to eighteen years old. Within a few years the original journal evolved into the more startlingly designed and expensively produced *Gioventù fascista* (Fascist youth), edited by the regime's leading ideologue, Achille Starace. Through its modernist, streamlined cover illustrations of young Vanguardisti, the magazine defined a graphic style that increased the party's allure and popularity among young people.

Boys as young as six years old were inducted into the Figli della Lupa (Sons of the She-Wolf), a name that referred to the legendary founders of Rome, Romulus and Remus, the abandoned sons of the war god Mars, who were adopted and suckled by a kindly she-wolf. Older boys, from eight to fourteen years old, graduated to the Opera Nazionale Balilla (National Balilla Organization—named after a young rebel who had given the signal for revolt against the occupying Austrians in 1746). Then came the Vanguardisti, which for a while was the last step before party membership. However, Mussolini believed that eighteen-year-olds were still too immature to be viable Fascist legionnaires, so in 1930 the Grand Fascist Council founded the Fasci Giovanili di Combattimento (Young Fascist Fighters) for boys eighteen to twenty-one, the ideological and military gateway for the new Fascist man. Girls had mirror organizations—young girls were invited into the Piccole Italiane (Little Italians); older girls belonged to the Giovani Italiane (Young Italians). These youth groups emphasized sports and martial training, with one aim: to prepare Italian youth for military service.

Youth groups swore an oath to Italy: "In the name of God and the Italian fatherland, in the name of all those who died for the greatness of Italy, I swear to consecrate myself, wholly and forever, to the good of Italy."[15] A key element of membership in Fascist organizations was the uniform, and certain days were set aside during the week when all were required to wear their uniforms in public. Along with the ubiquitous images of Il Duce and the *fascio*, the party uniform was a centerpiece of Fascist style, seen on banners, signs, and billboards. Photographs of

172. *Gioventù Italiana del Littorio* (Italian Youth of the Littorio) This back cover of a *quaderno* (student assignment book) represents a member of the Fasci Giovanili. 1930

173. *GIL Anno XX* (GIL year 20) The Ministero dell'Educazione Nazionale issued report cards for the Gioventù Italiana del Littorio (GIL) youth organization, with front and back covers replete with Fascist military symbols. 1942

Background: Young Italian gymnasts during a display in front of Mussolini in Rome. 15 September 1936

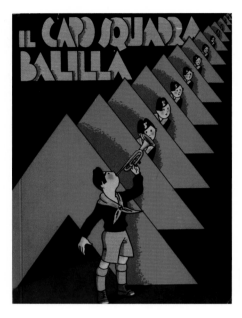

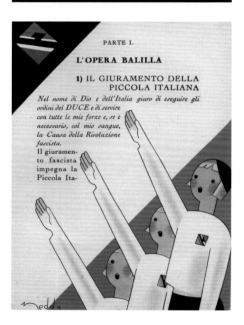

uniformed troops appeared in every newspaper and magazine, and newsreels showed legions of soldiers marching in *passo romano*. These images conveyed one reality, while another portrayed individual young Fascists in sleek poses, like statues poured in a perfect mold. The airbrush became an ideological tool; Fascist artists used it to streamline human figures into modernistic effigies, creating an image of the Giovanili as the perfect manifestation of obedience and allegiance.

Parallel to the youth organizations was a new education system conceived as early as 1923 by education minister and Fascist philosopher Giovanni Gentile to turn youth into instruments of the regime. Education became a tool for molding the Fascist conscience and Fascist will. The strategy was an aggressive attempt to inculcate, primarily in male youngsters, the myth of the omnipotent regime in order to transform so-called Flowers of Faith into soldiers of empire. As Il Duce consolidated power, the party increased the role of Fascist organizations such as the Balilla and Giovanili in the educational system, and teachers were required to influence pupils to join Fascist youth organizations. Textbooks combining conventional studies and party requisites were illustrated with Fascist images. School identity cards, educational certificates, diplomas, and *quaderni* were colorfully designed with Fascist emblems: imperial eagles, stylized daggers, and even silhouettes of Il Duce. Fascist iconography permeated the students' daily lives. Teachers were given the task of glorifying Mussolini on all occasions, and all classes started the day singing Fascist hymns such as "Giovinezza" and "Balilla," the anthems of the youth organizations.

Fascist doctrine was also aggressively promoted through the universities. Once the anti-Fascist professors had been removed from their posts, all teachers were ordered to wear uniforms while on duty. In 1924 the Gruppi Universitari Fascisti (GUF;

176

177

178

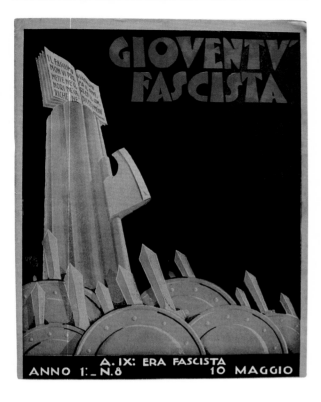

179–82. *Gioventù fascista*
(Fascist youth)
This official magazine,
edited by Achille
Starace, was Mussolini's
constant link to the
Vanguardisti. Early
issues illustrated by
Cesare Gobbo empha-
sized speed, a key
tenet of the Futurists,
and power, the principle
behind Fascism
(179–82).
1931

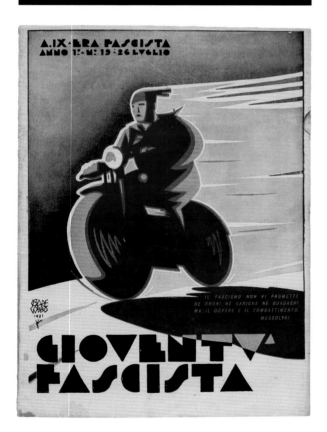

183

184

185

186

183–86. *Gioventù fascista*
(Fascist youth)
Each issue was
introduced by Mussolini
and featured stories
of Fascist military and
paramilitary heroism,
and how good work
was the foundation of
the Fascist New Man.
While the interior
design was fairly
conventional, the covers
represented Fascism
as a progressive,
dynamic force leading
Italy into the future.
The covers featured
here were illustrated by
Mario Sironi (183), and
unidentified designers
(184–86). Later issues
were designed in
a manner similar to
many commercial
magazines, with duotone
photographs like the
one of Il Duce feeding
chickens (186).
1931–35

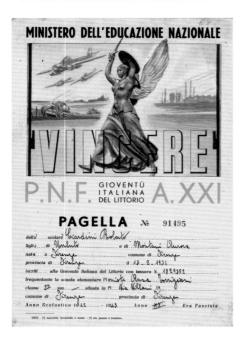

University Fascist Group) was established, and students flocked to it, largely because membership secured certain privileges from the state but also, one suspects, for the regalia it offered.

The Fascists tightened their hold on youth in part through that most visible of symbols, the uniform. Fascist garb was paramount in establishing both conformity and an elite within Italian society. Uniforms were designed with careful attention to detail and style; the regalia (including shiny badges and insignia) increased in direct proportion to completed indoctrination. Uniforms were required at all official youth group meetings (of which there were many), as well as at all rites and celebrations. Although uniforms were not compulsory for every student during school hours, those without them were suspect.

In contrast to the ponderous Heroic Realism of Nazi iconography, portrayals of Fascist youth favored the Futurist style, which streamlined the human figure essentially to a sleek logo, much as in commercial advertising at the time. Consequently, the quintessential Balilla member—wearing short pants, black shirt, fez, and crossed blue neckerchief— looked more like a toy soldier than a young boy, while the helmeted Vanguardisto, carrying baton or dagger, looked more menacing, caught between youth and adulthood. Members of the Giovanili were often portrayed holding weapons as they thrust forward in lockstep formation, symbolic of the perpetual motion underscoring the Fascist myth.

Quaderni were so common that they were ideally suited to the daily reinforcement of Fascist doctrine, and they offer telling examples of the hybrid Fascist graphic style. Some covers show the Roman *fascio* rendered in a classical manner, while others mix ancient with Moderne renderings. The most popular *quaderni* covers depict warplanes, weapons, and scenes of Fascist conquest (particularly in Abyssinia), sometimes drawn in a light-handed cartoon style,

187. Report card
The Fascist party issued *pagella* (report cards) to all members of its youth organization, the Gioventù Italiana del Littorio (GIL), featuring graphics celebrating Italy's new empire. 1943

188. Diploma
Official documents, like this diploma of admission to the Ente Nazionale per l'Insegnamento Medio e Superiore (middle school), were often illustrated (in this case by C.V. Testi) with regal symbols. 1933

189–94. *Dall'A alla Z*
(From A to Z)
The Fascists injected their history into all educational materials. This profusely illustrated A to Z of the party was aimed at preteen Italian boys who were ripe for the Balilla. 1934

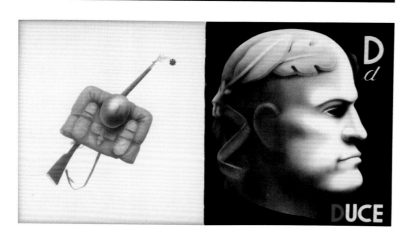

often with the motto "Mussolini is always right" emblazoned on the front or back.

Although Mussolini used the Roman heritage and some of its imperialist trappings as a cornerstone of Fascist style, he did not sacrifice the sense of modernity that appealed to the young. Most of the publications aimed at young Fascists were in a modernist style. *Il capo squadra Balilla* (The leader of the Balilla squadron), a handbook for little Fascists, features colorful drawings of young boys illustrated in a modern style. Party slogans and mottos are set in angular type to give the impression that they are being screamed across the page. Magazine and book covers, posters, and countless other ephemera designed for the Vanguardisti and Giovanili were printed in bright colors and streamlined letters that echo the vibrant designs by the Futurist Fortunato Depero. Unlike the solemn Nazi style used for similar purposes, Italian graphics retained a certain exuberance in works designed for the young.

propaganda power

The Fascists established control over newspapers and newsreels very early on. The daily press was congenial to Fascists because many of the *vecchia guardia* (old guard), including Mussolini, had begun as writers or journalists. The Fascists not only controlled Mussolini's own newspaper, *Il popolo d'Italia*, and later *La rivista illustrata del popolo d'Italia* (Illustrated review of the people of Italy), the paper's popular illustrated magazine supplement, they bought shares in many daily and weekly newspapers; by 1934 they owned 66 percent of all national and local newspapers. After 1924 the party issued daily instructions to the newspapers, directing how Il Duce and Fascist events should be covered, and they closed down any periodical that tainted the image of the regime. In addition to the general press, scores of literary, scientific, and art periodicals supported Mussolini through word and image, and proffered Fascist theories.

Tapping into new media technologies was also inevitable for the modern dictatorship. Although Mussolini preferred speaking directly to audiences from his balcony at the Palazzo Venezia in Rome, he knew the value of radio and film in reaching the masses. In 1925 the government established an institute for propaganda through cinematography, called LUCE, meaning "light," the acronym for L'Unione Cinematografica Educativa (Union of Educational Cinema). LUCE produced *Chronicle del regime* (Chronicle of the regime), a daily review of Fascist achievements that all cinemas had to show prior to the feature presentation or risk losing their license. In 1936 Mussolini decided to take control of nonpolitical films, too—primarily for the revenue stream but also to have additional brand placement opportunities for Fascist ideology. He personally laid the foundation stone of Cinecittà (Film City) outside Rome, and placed his son Vittorio in charge

195–202. *Quaderni* (assignment booklets) Schoolchildren used *quaderni* for reports and exams. It was the perfect vehicle for illustrated propaganda designed to herald the glories of the Fascist empire, the duties of young Fascists, and the camaraderie between Fascists old and young. 1919–40

203–5. *Gruppi Universitari Fascisti* (GUF; University Fascist Group) This catalog describes the virtues of being a member of the GUF, which prepared university students for the Fascist party. It cleverly modernized imperial symbols to conflate history and progress. 1933

Background: Young Fascist youth organization in Northern Italy. 1927

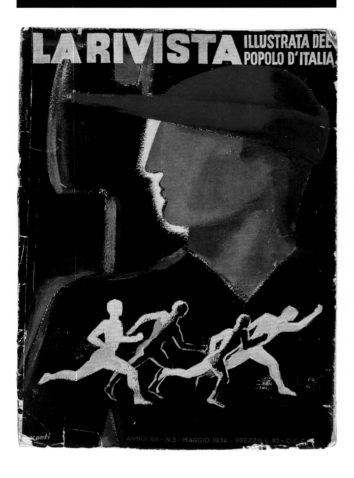

206–7. *La rivista illustrata del popolo d'Italia* (Illustrated review of the people of Italy) This stunningly designed weekly supplement to Mussolini's newspaper, *Il popolo d'Italia*, was edited by Arnaldo Mussolini and Manlio Morgagni. It catered to a general audience with stories about contemporary life in Italy. Though its covers were usually propagandistic, they were not necessarily pedantic. Many issues were designed by leading artists, such as Xanti Schawinsky (206) and Fortunato Depero (207). 1934–35

of the complex. (Despite its Fascist origins, Cinecittà today is the Hollywood of Italy, and legendary among movie fans as the birthplace of Italian New Wave cinema.)

Much of the regime's propaganda was controlled through Giovanni Gentile's Istituto Fascista di Cultura (Fascist Cultural Institute). Based in Rome, with branches in other major cities, the institute promoted Fascism to the more cultivated sectors of Italian life. It made certain that libraries had a full complement of sanctioned Fascist literature, and it scheduled Fascist lectures throughout Italy. In 1937 the institute was merged with the Press and Propaganda Office into the Ministero della Cultura Popolare (Ministry for Popular Culture), which controlled the press, film, and book publishing—in short, the regime's communication tools.

Italian poster design was among the most striking in Europe before World War II. The Fascist

movement initially managed to seduce artists with its innovative ideas and ambiguous political message (before Fascist rhetoric became exacerbated by the influence of Nazism). Paolo Garretto, a Naples-born caricaturist and poster artist, was one of the leading proponents of Art Moderne. Influenced by Cubism and Futurism, his flat, streamlined style was decidedly hybrid. Well known throughout Italy for his covers for fashion magazines like *Adam*, he also regularly illustrated covers for the American magazines *Fortune* and *Vanity Fair*, and made caricatures for *Vogue* and portraits for the *New Yorker*. Although much of his work was apolitical, his close ties to Fascism later had repercussions for his career. At the age of eighteen Garretto, who hated the Bolsheviks for having attacked his liberal father on the street, joined the Vanguardisti. Soon after, he was brought to the attention of Mussolini for having taken it upon himself to redesign the Fascist uniform. (Garretto said he

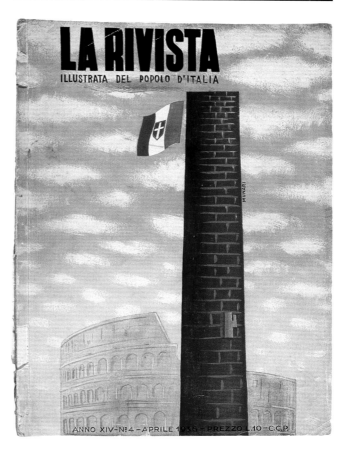

208–9. *La rivista illustrata del popolo d'Italia* (Illustrated review of the people of Italy)
These covers were designed by Mario Sironi (208) and Bruno Munari (209). 1935–36

disliked the uncoordinated attire of Fascist militia officers.) When Il Duce saw him and a few of his cohorts in formation, dressed in their smart new coordinated black garb, he promptly appointed them to his personal bodyguard detachment. This seemed a great honor, until Garretto learned that the position was for life. He managed to get out of service, but continued to produce artwork for the Italian press.

By the 1930s Garretto was one of the best-known poster artists in Europe and New York, sought after by many publishers and advertising agencies. His satiric caricatures of Mussolini and Hitler for *Vanity Fair* strained his ties to the Fascist party, and he was given a contract by *Harper's Bazaar* editor Carmel Snow to do ten covers; only one was completed, however, and it never ran. When the war broke out, Snow canceled Garretto's contract because of his Fascist ties. In 1941 he was interned in the United States with other "enemy aliens," then eventually deported to Italy, with

the unenforceable proviso that he not make any anti-American artwork for the duration of the war. In 1944 he took an assignment to go to Budapest to develop a literacy project so that "defeated and conquered peoples" could learn the Italian language through pictures. When Italy capitulated to the Allies later that year, he was interned as an enemy alien in Hungary until the end of the war.

Some modernist images were rooted in the Italian vernacular. While adhering to a national graphic style, artists were nevertheless encouraged to exploit the styles of their regions. Fortunato Depero, for instance, reinterpreted a Mediterranean aesthetic that borrowed from the pottery and fabric found near his home town of Rovereto.

Mario Sironi, another stalwart of Fascist style, was primarily a painter (his work frequently appeared on covers of *La rivista*) and art critic for *Il popolo d'Italia*, who designed an extensive exhibition and

catalog of Fascism's first ten years. Sironi's design celebrated the marriage of Fascist modernism and classicism, while at the same time paying homage to the events (and violence) that had brought the movement to power. In one room he designed multiple columns of Art Moderne *fasci,* the cantilevered blades forming a kind of triumphal arch. On the walls, the forced perspectives of the emblems and flags suggested the height of modernity, and the dramatic lighting further added to its monumentality. Even in photographs his design acuity is impressive.

Art Moderne and Futurism were effective graphic styles when Italian Fascism was still relatively untainted. In the early years, when Fascism still appeared to be improving the Italian standard of living, a relatively soft-sell graphic approach lulled the citizenry into a sense of patriotic delight. But when Mussolini (once praised as Europe's peacemaker for staving off Hitler's early aggressions) began his own brutal imperialist pursuits in the mid-1930s, hard-sell graphics figured more prominently in the propaganda strategy. The debacle of the Italian military in Northern Africa notwithstanding, poster

campaigns began using heroic graphics that unambiguously celebrated victory. By the advent of World War II, Italy's graphic style was not very different from that of Nazi Germany—or, for that matter, from standard American and English propaganda images. And during the war, as Italian soldiers were being shipped home in coffins from abroad or dying on native soil, the propaganda machine pumped out graphics with only one true goal—to convince the masses that all was not lost, although it was.

210–13. *Mostra della rivoluzione fascista* (Exhibition of the Fascist revolution)
The Fascists made events like this exhibition in commemoration of the tenth anniversary of the Fascist revolution into a traveling spectacle. The cover of a small booklet of train tickets reproduces art by Mario Sironi, the designer of the installation (210); the back cover for the exhibition catalog creates a typographic image with the X (for ten years) superimposed on the syllables *du-ce*, giving the impression that the Italian leader's name is chanted in cadence (211); the premiere of the exhibition at the Palazzo delle Esposizioni in Rome featured a building facade composed of mammoth *fasci* and huge block letters designed by architects Mario de Renzi and Adalberto Libera. Noteworthy for its dramatic lighting, the interior design included photomontage and large typographic displays by Mario Sironi and Enrico Prampolini. 1932

death to mussolini

In 1943, after the Allied invasion of Sicily, the Fascist regime collapsed. Mussolini fled to Germany and was soon installed as dictator of the Italian Social Republic, a small puppet state based in Salò on Lake Garda. Its flag featured the Italian colors of red, white, and green, with an eagle holding a *fascio* in its talons. By then, however, Mussolini was virtually powerless. In the south, the visual legacy of Fascism was systematically destroyed by the angry populace.

Mussolini was shot on 28 April 1945. The next day, his body was exhibited next to that of his mistress, Clara Petacci, and other Fascists in the Piazzale Loreto in Milan, hung from an Esso gas station. The display of the bodies signified the completion of the Fascist narrative: Here ended the story of a man who had styled himself as a myth, and whose regime relied upon the power of design to seduce its followers. The public display was deemed necessary to dispel the myth of Il Duce's invincibility. Arguably, he should have been brought to trial—but the potential for his martyrdom was judged unacceptable. The display of his body in such an extraordinary manner, amid the banal landscape of a war-torn city (at a gas station, no less), was, in a sense, the perfect end to Fascist dominance.

Photographs of the event, widely distributed at the time, were cropped to focus on Mussolini with the stalwart Petacci and one of the four other Fascists who were hung alongside them. At the time, the image provoked chills of joy—as with those of other defeated dictators whose corpses became icons of victory. However, unlike the situation in Germany after defeat, symbols of Fascism in Italy were not outlawed. And today, a semiofficial shrine erected to Mussolini in his hometown in Predappio, Italy, still attracts many visitors every year.

Fascist style predated National Socialist style by a decade but was ultimately less effective as a consistent brand. Thanks to the early alliance with the Futurists, Fascist aesthetics transcended its political roots and ultimately had a strong influence on European graphic design.

Opposite:
This "U.S. Official Photograph No. RA. 14164," distributed by the Office of War Information, titled *Ignominy,* shows a soldier of the Fifth Army looking at a huge portrait of the fallen dictator after the Allied invasion of Anzio. 13 February 1944

the soviet communists

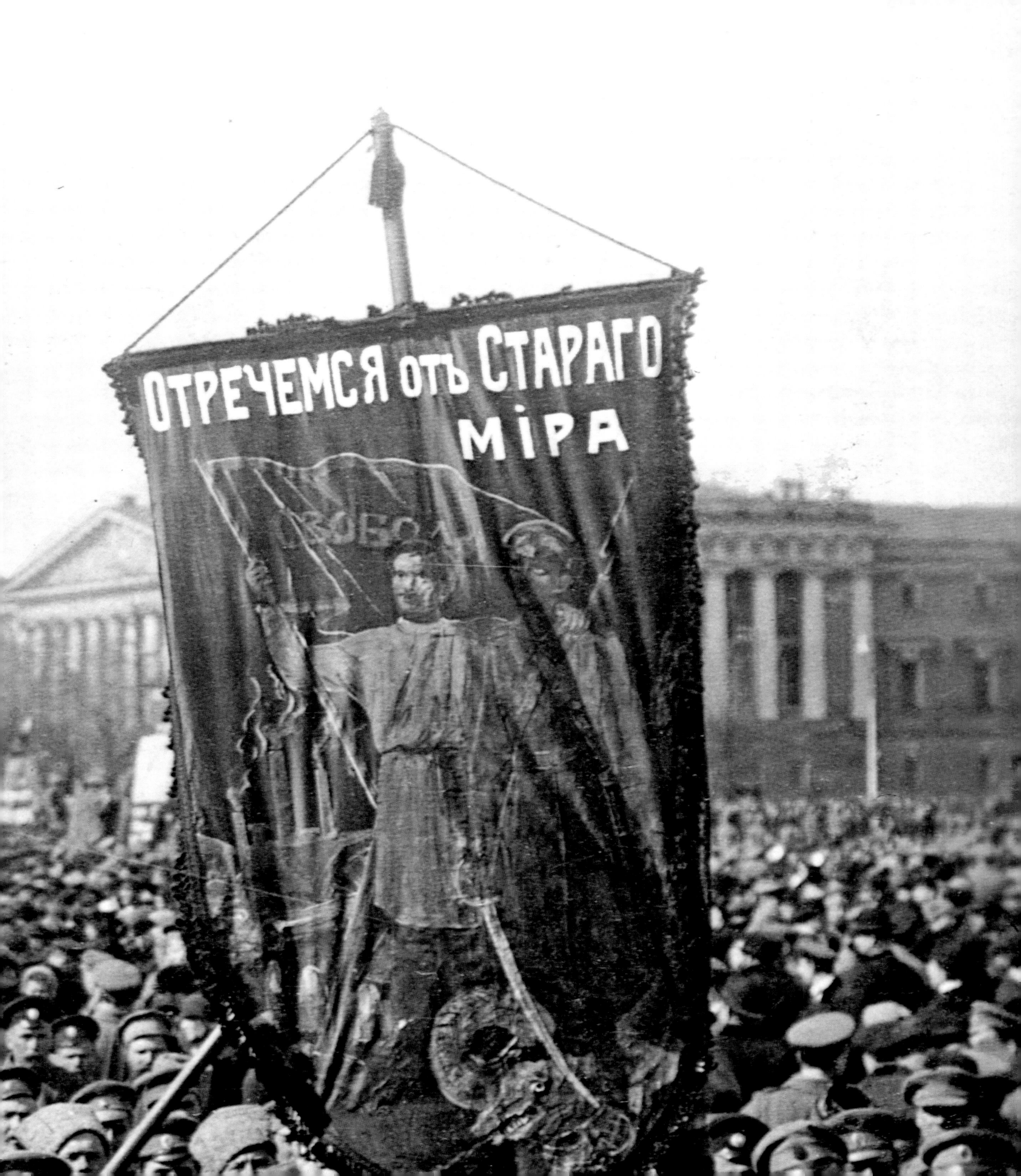
ОТРЕЧЕМСЯ отъ СТАРАГО
МІРА

branding marxism

[Socialist Realism] demands of the artist the truthful, historically concrete representation of reality in its revolutionary development. Moreover, the truthfulness and historical concreteness of the artistic representation of reality must be linked with the task of ideological transformation and education of workers in the spirit of socialism.
—from the *Statute of the Union of Soviet Writers*, 1934

naming the revolution

The term Bolshevik was coined at the Second Congress of the Russian Social Democratic Workers' party (RSDWP) in 1903. The word derives from the Russian word *bol'she*, meaning "bigger" or "more," and referred to the majority faction within the RSDWP led by Vladimir Ilich Ulyanov, otherwise known by his revolutionary name, V. I. Lenin, pitted in ideological battle against the smaller faction referred to as the Mensheviks (*Men'sheviki*, from the Russian *men'she*, "less" or "few"). The earth-shattering revolution of 1917 that deposed the czar and brought the Bolshevik faction to power became known as the Bolshevik revolution, and the term quickly gained international notoriety. During the interwar years it was commonly used by right-wing politicians to denigrate left-wing movements in Europe, and it is still sometimes used as a derogatory term to designate extreme left-wing ideas. In Russia, however, the RSDWP was renamed the Russian Communist party just six months after the 1917 revolution, and "Bolshevik" was completely dropped as an official term in 1952.

Soviet is the Russian word for "council" or "advice." The term was first used politically in 1905, when workers organized themselves into the Soviet of Workers' Deputies to coordinate revolutionary activities against the czar, but the workers were defeated by the regime and the soviets suppressed. In 1917 a spontaneous revolution erupted against the czarist regime in protest against the terrible economic conditions linked to Russia's mishandled efforts in World War I. The czar abdicated in February, leading to a relative power vacuum despite the formation of a moderate provisional government. The soviets reconvened, and in June convoked the first All-Russian Congress. By October, the Bolsheviks had gained a majority in the soviets, and during the "ten days that shook the world" (as American journalist John Reed famously dubbed it),[1] Lenin's faction overthrew the provisional government, and the Soviet Congress, dominated by Lenin's Bolshevik faction, took over power in Russia. Soviet Russia became the Union of Soviet Socialist Republics (USSR) when four Soviet Socialist Republics—Russian, Transcaucasian, Ukrainian, and Byelorussian—merged together in 1922. SSRs were subsequently added, to a total of fifteen, until the disintegration of the USSR in 1991.

the use of emblems

The ruling Russian feudal families and the czarist regime had revelled in Russian national symbols such as the imperial double-headed eagle, Saint George slaying the dragon, and the cross of Saint Andrew. When the Bolsheviks seized power, they rejected such iconic trappings as aristocratic folly and superstitious authoritarianism, in keeping with the orthodox Marxist view that political symbols are designed to

214. Soviet flag
The red flag with a yellow star and hammer and sickle, symbolizing the unity of workers and peasants.
Date unknown

Background:
Lenin addresses the crowd in a public square in Moscow.
c. 1920

Previous spread:
May Day celebration in Petrograd.
1 May 1917

trick the population into submission. Symbols, Karl Marx believed, fail to contribute to a true understanding of issues; he considered them dangerous in that they substituted an ideal for the real, a false front for an honest social dynamic. In his analysis, symbols perpetuated fictions that had been manufactured to promote the feudal system. He wrote that symbolism "is a political subterfuge that is consciously or unconsciously created for the sake of dominance."[2]

In 1917 the Soviet leaders rejected the notion of state symbols. In their view, the inevitability of a worldwide proletarian revolution obviated the need for nationalist branding. The Russian revolutionary flags and banners were simply blood red. As early as the fifteenth century, the red flag was a symbol of defiance for kings and princes under attack, signaling that they would not surrender and that no prisoners would be taken alive.[3] The Jacobins used red in the French Revolution, and during the nineteenth century red became the color of socialism, culminating as the symbol for the historic uprising of the Paris Commune. Red, the color adopted by the Bolsheviks, was initially the sole emblem of the Communist state.

Shifting from their purist stance with regard to imagery, Soviet leaders adopted state symbols when they founded the USSR in 1922. Article 22 of the Treaty Concerning the Formation of the Union of Soviet Socialist Republics stated that the Soviet Union "shall have its own flag, coat of arms, and state seal." The red flag became the symbol of the state, with a yellow star—whose five points represent the unity of peoples on five continents—and the hammer and sickle (originally designed in 1918 as a more cumbersome hammer and plow) representing the unity of the workers and peasants. The Soviet Union also adopted a separate coat of arms and a state seal, whose ornate design recalls czarist emblems. The imperial seal was surrounded by a laurel including the coats of arms of the different aristocratic families, with the crown atop the symbol of Saint George representing supreme czarist power.[4] The central figure of the Soviet state emblem is a globe, colored yellow for the land masses and blue for the oceans, over which are imposed a gold hammer and sickle. Above the Russia-centered world, which is illuminated by a rising sun, is a yellow and red five-pointed star. The whole is surrounded by a wreath made of wheat tied with a red ribbon, annotated with the rallying cry "Workers of the World Unite."

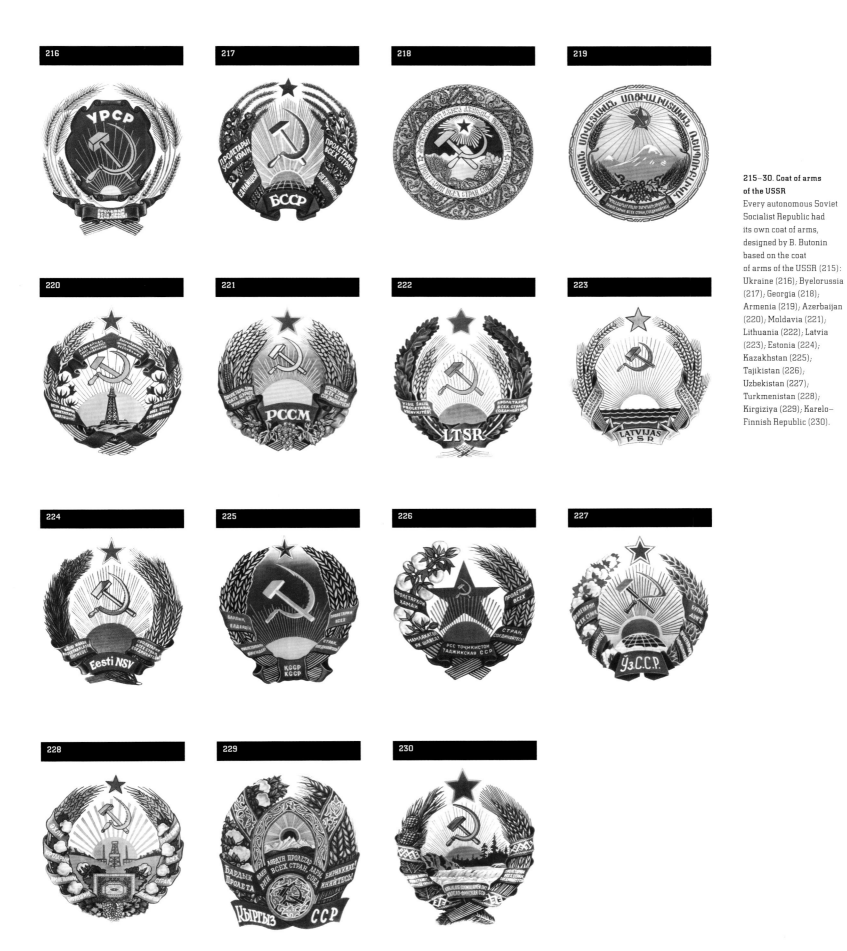

215–30. Coat of arms
of the USSR
Every autonomous Soviet
Socialist Republic had
its own coat of arms,
designed by B. Butonin
based on the coat
of arms of the USSR (215):
Ukraine (216); Byelorussia
(217); Georgia (218);
Armenia (219); Azerbaijan
(220); Moldavia (221);
Lithuania (222); Latvia
(223); Estonia (224);
Kazakhstan (225);
Tajikistan (226);
Uzbekistan (227);
Turkmenistan (228);
Kirgiziya (229); Karelo–
Finnish Republic (230).

the soviet avant-garde

inadvertent allies: the avant-garde

The artistic and literary avant-gardes that had been emerging in Russia long before 1917 played a very influential role in the revolution, both actively and inadvertently, but were later completely eradicated.

Lenin's stance on art's role in society had evolved over the course of many years. In his 1905 essay "Party Organization and Party Literature" (which served as the blueprint for Mao Zedong's concept of "state art"), Lenin addressed the place of literature and journalism in the state he foresaw, and he also spoke broadly of art's role in the burgeoning party: "We want to establish, and shall establish, a free press, free not simply from the police but also from capital, careerism, and moreover, from bourgeois-anarchist individualism." The essay touted art as a tool needed to finish what the Bolsheviks had started. "The revolution is not completed," Lenin warned. "While tzarism is *no longer* strong enough to defeat the revolution, the revolution is *not yet* strong enough to defeat tzarism."[5] The concerted efforts of loyal writers and artists would be essential to achieving victory.

Hitler, Mussolini, and Mao were self-styled "artists"; Lenin was not. His concern with art was limited to practical matters. The strict Soviet art and design policies were not formulated until a decade after his death, the brainchild of Iosif Vissarionovich Dzhugashvili—better known as Joseph Stalin. But, as historian Matthew Cullerne Bown notes, "Lenin's few interventions into cultural life are still very significant in that they foreshadowed much of what was to follow after his death.... Official Stalinist art was a legitimate child of Lenin's revolution."[6]

The movement known as Proletkult (from *proletarskaya kultura*, or proletarian culture) exemplifies early Bolshevik attempts to revolutionize art.[7] Although Lenin was opposed to this idea— believing that the masses required cultural authoritarianism rather than collective art experience— the movement nonetheless flourished until the early 1920s. The aim of the Proletkult was to expunge elitist art by encouraging the proletariat to participate in the conception of production art—the creation of functional artifacts for everyday life—through a network of schools and workshops created all over Russia. The Proletkult also fought illiteracy. By 1920 there were at least 400,000 members in art studios and clubs,[8] and twenty Proletkult journals analyzed the process of creating revolutionary art. Until they were dissolved in 1932, the Proletkult organizations were a wellspring of progressive Communist ideals, rooted in Lenin's idea that art must conform to the principle of *partiinost*, total submission to the party and state.

The avant-garde flourished in Russia at the beginning of the twentieth century, first with the Russian Cubo-Futurist art movement, and then with the more radically abstract Suprematist

231. Odessa
Travel poster done in Art Deco style to appeal to foreign tourists.
c. 1928

232. Soviet theater
This special issue of *SSSR Umění* (USSR art) was designed by Jiří Friml and produced in Czechoslovkia.
1935

Background:
Workers carrying placards in procession during Red Week in Moscow.
1924

movement originated by Kazimir Malevich around 1913. This unprecedented combination of pure geometry and minimalist color palette defined the modernist visual foundation upon which Russian Constructivism, and European modernism, would be built. Progressive Russian artists viewed the Bolshevik revolution as an opportunity to expand art beyond antiquated (and bourgeois) notions of representation.

Many artists believed art should serve the regime and voluntarily joined state-run arts organizations, where, for a time, they enjoyed artistic freedom. Under Anatoly Vasilyevich Lunacharsky (a former exile and cofounder of the Proletkult), the art department

of Narkompros (Commissariat for Enlightenment) became a wellspring of cultural activity. During his time as head of Narkompros, Lunacharsky was instrumental in enabling avant-garde artists to work until it was politically imprudent to do so, and helped to save historic works of art and architecture from destruction. He also played an important role in education reform, leading the first major campaign against adult illiteracy. In 1929 he was placed in charge of the state's censorship apparatus; as the avant-garde was scrutinized, this involved curtailing cultural activities—including art, music, dance, film—that appeared to have agendas not entirely dedicated to

233–44. Rosta window posters These posters designed by Vladimir Lebedev were created for Rosta, the Russian Telegraph Agency, which commissioned well-known artists such as Lebedev, Mikhail Cheremnykh, Vladimir Mayakovsky, and Alexander Rodchenko to design so-called window posters to be hung in shop windows across Russia. 1920–21

the state. When Stalin consolidated his power in the late 1920s, Lunacharsky was removed from his post (although not from the party; he was later appointed ambassador to the League of Nations and to Spain).

In large part owing to Lunacharsky's efforts, academic art institutions—the same ones that had vehemently rejected the avant-garde prior to the Bolshevik revolution—were closed down in the wake of the October Revolution and reorganized into so-called State Free Art Studios. These offered open access to all students—irrespective of their artistic education or skill—to continue the battle against any vestige of czarist elitism. All artistic viewpoints, from Cubism

to realism, were propounded at these workshops. Students were not indoctrinated in one particular "revolutionary" art genre, and discussions arose among students over what was the most appropriate Soviet style. The proponents of "agitation art" (or agitprop) formed into Obmokhu (Society of Young Artists) in 1919, its mission being to produce posters and banners for social causes. To demonstrate the importance of their collective work, the acronym Obmokhu replaced any personal signatures on their work.

Constructivist artist-designer Alexander Rodchenko, who applied his talents to state propaganda, said in 1921, "It is time for art to flow into the organization of life."[9] The Productivist movement, created by a group of Constructivist artists, including Rodchenko, believed that functional design should contribute to building the Communist world. Productivists sought to forge close ties between art and industry (as did the German Bauhaus) in order to produce wares designed to enhance the lives of the working class. The concept of "production art" was consistent with Lenin's plan to regenerate the Soviet economy, and particularly its industry. Its merits were discussed in the pages of the official Narkompros magazine *Iskusstvo kommuny* (Art of the commune). Emphasis was placed on breaking down barriers between art and work, art and life, art and production. From these discussions emerged Inkhuk (Institute of Artistic Culture). Established as the theoretical arm of Narkompros, Inkhuk was devoted to creating an infrastructure in which artists were trained to produce proletarian design. It analyzed how modern art could serve the state's Marxist materialist theories.

A third key institution was established to provide practical training in textile design, ceramics, architecture, woodwork, metalwork, and graphic arts. Vkhutemas (Higher Art and Technical Studios), founded in Moscow in 1920, was open to the proletariat but not to the bourgeoisie. For nearly ten years after the revolution, Vkhutemas produced a considerable amount of experimental "new Soviet" art—abstract, Suprematist, Constructivist—but functional design, which was seen as contributing to the state's industrialization plan, was uppermost on the agenda.

revolutionary posters

The poster was one of the most spontaneous artistic manifestations of the revolution, and it was central to defining the iconography of the period until 1927, by which point Stalin had secured control of the state and eliminated his political rivals. Thousands of posters were designed by both veteran and unknown artists and produced by official organizations, among them Rosta (the Russian Telegraph Agency), the State Publishing House, the Political Directorates of the Reserve Army, the Central Directorate of Cooperatives, and the Moscow Committee of the Russian Communist party. Many posters incorporated caricatures stylistically similar to drawings dating from the European revolutions of 1848 and the Paris Commune and influenced by the Russian *lubok*, a type of satirical color prints popular during Czar Nicholas's reign.

One of the best-known posters, Rodchenko's 1924 *Books*, is considered a classic example of Constructivist graphic design. By establishing an unprecedented form language not seen in other European countries, it contributed greatly to the new visual identity of the Soviet state. El Lissitzky's 1919 *Beat the Whites with the Red Wedge* is a brilliant example of Suprematist abstraction used as political polemic. Dmitry Moor's 1920 *Have You Volunteered?* (influenced by early World War I British recruiting posters featuring Lord Kitchener, as well as the famous American army recruitment poster, James Montgomery Flagg's 1917 *I Want You!*) is a more traditional academic rendering. Other poster images ran the gamut from nineteenth-century representational lithographic crayon drawing to high-contrast posterized graphics to Cubo-Futurist styling. The poet and artist Vladimir Mayakovsky invented an entirely new style of so-called posters for Rosta: cartoonish glyphs composed in a sequential manner with stencil-like writing below, which hung in telegraph offices throughout Russia.

Bolsheviks used posters as a call to arms during the revolution; after the revolution, posters carried slogans touting "general peace." With the outbreak of the Russian Civil War after the Bolsheviks signed the Brest-Litovsk treaty in 1918, posters attacked counterrevolutionaries and the White Guards.

245. *Books*
Alexander Rodchenko's
famous poster was
created for Lengiz, the
Leningrad branch
of the State publishing
house. It reads "Lengiz:
books in all branches
of knowledge."
1924

246. *Beat the Whites
with the Red Wedge*
El Lissitzky's poster
was created during the
Russian Civil War
between the Communists
(the Reds) and their
opponents (the Whites).
1919

247. Let's build
a fleet of airships in
Lenin's name
Georgii Kibardin's
poster, which
combines drawing
and photography, is
a classic example
of postrevolutionary
Russian posters.
1931

248. Let us fulfill the
plan of great works
This montage poster by
Gustav Klucis promoted
the Soviet Union's
First Five-Year Plan.
1930

249. *Crocodile*
Founded in 1922, this was a Communist party–sanctioned satiric journal. This cover takes aim at the Nazis and imperial Japan. 1941

250–51. *Godless at the Workbench*
Dmitry Moor was the art director of this atheist magazine, published by the Moscow branch of the Communist party from 1923 to 1931. 1927–29

252–55. *USSR in Construction*
This magazine, published in five languages for an international market, promoted the nation's industrial and agricultural accomplishments. Issues based on specific themes were designed by prominent designers such as Natan Altman (252–53), El Lissitzky (254), and Alexander Rodchenko (255) for an issue devoted to the poet Vladimir Mayakovsky. 1930–40

By 1920 the Whites were more or less crushed. Attention turned to the New Economic Policy (NEP), with which, in order to rebuild the Soviet economy, Lenin allowed a modicum of private ownership of factories and farms. Posters promised reconstruction, education, and collectivization, and even made appeals to combat anti-Semitism. Even though there was no overarching poster campaign, the cumulative impact of these posters fostered a visual identity for the revolutionary state before more rigid artistic guidelines were imposed.

photomontage and film

Photography, and particularly photomontage, was a defining medium of the Soviet style. One of the innovators, the Constructivist artist Gustav Klucis, developed a unique form of political photomontage that involved layering typography and photography to create dynamic asymmetrical compositions. A one-time student of Kazimir Malevich, Klucis considered traditional art—drawing, painting, graphic art— to be obsolete and unsuitable for political propaganda on a mass scale. Photomontage allowed Klucis to juxtapose images freely for maximum psychological impact while using a medium that gave the illusion of reality. The use of the camera, an art machine for

a machine age, underscored Lenin's wish to propel the Soviet Union into the industrial age, and Klucis brilliantly used photographs to conflate different realities into one image. Other leading photomontage artists who engaged in typofoto (the marriage of typography and photographic image) included Alexander Rodchenko, who produced posters for films, department stores, and literature, and the Stenberg brothers, Georgii and Vladimir, known for their film advertisements. The Soviet-style montage would come to define the era and was hugely influential outside the Soviet Union. The manipulated photograph allowed for a new kind of propaganda that wedded truth to fantasy to convey a utopian ideal.

Motion pictures also served as an invaluable propaganda tool. Films, like photomontage, presented an illusion of reality. Lenin approved of cinema for conveying information while entertaining the masses. Sergei Eisenstein's propaganda films of the 1920s—*Strike*, *Battleship Potemkin*, and *October* among them—made groundbreaking use of montage and innovative film editing. Linking brief scenes in a series of related quick-cut shots, Eisenstein juxtaposed images to manipulate the emotions of his audience in ways that art or literature could not. Having studied earlier expressionistic filmmakers, he used surreal and expressive techniques to condense complex stories

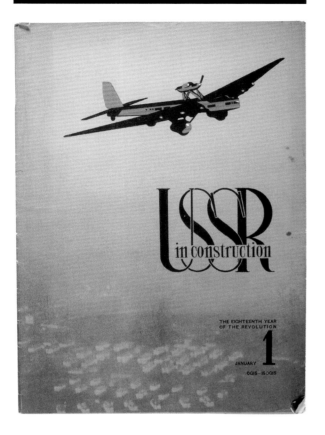

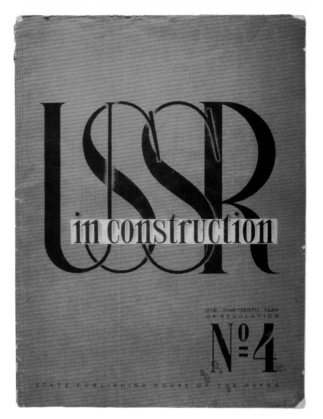

256–67. *USSR in Construction*
The tenth issue of this magazine, designed by El Lissitzky, was devoted to Stalin's push to make electric power available everywhere in the Soviet Union. Lissitzky combined manipulated and unadulterated documentary photographs (by Max Alpert) to create cinematic animation on the printed page. 1932

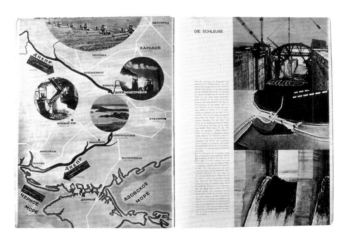

268. *Illustrierte Geschichte der russischen Revolution* (Illustrated history of the Russian revolution) This publication, designed by the German montagist John Heartfield for a German Communist publisher, is bathed in red, the color of the Communist revolution. 1927

269. *Where the Workers Are in Power* Red is again the dominant hue on Varvara Stepanova's cover for this pamphlet, published by the Cooperative Publishing Society of Foreign Workers in Moscow. 1931

into a few scenes. Eisenstein's work focused on class conflict, and employed nonactors to give his stories greater verisimilitude. Although he was employed by the Central Committee of the Communist party for a while, his films did not fit squarely into the Stalinist idea; as Socialist Realism grew more pervasive, Eisenstein found it harder to make films for the Soviet film industry. By the time *October* was released in 1928, all scenes featuring Trotsky and other leaders who had fallen to Stalin's purges were deleted. At a time when the avant-garde was on the wane and Stalin sought to invent his own myths, Eisenstein's progressive, metaphoric approach conflicted with Stalin's desire for more direct propagandistic messages. Unable to achieve his artistic vision, Eisenstein left for the United States. After a disastrous collaboration with Upton Sinclair in Mexico, Eisenstein returned to Russia, where he made *Alexander Nevsky*, his first sound film, in 1938. In 1945, part 1 of *Ivan the Terrible*

won the Stalin Prize, but in 1946 part 2 presented a more sinister view of Ivan's reign, which evoked Stalin's regime. Most of the footage for part 3 was destroyed, and Eisenstein died shortly afterward, in 1948.

international propaganda

From the outset, the Soviet regime worked to propagate the revolution outside its borders through magazines, books, and exhibitions designed by Russian avant-gardists—Constructivists and Productivists—including El Lissitzky, Alexander Rodchenko, Varvara Stepanova, Alexei Gan, Osip Brik, and Vladimir Tatlin.

Magazines like *USSR in Construction* celebrated the technological, industrial, agrarian, and cultural achievements of the Soviet state. *USSR in Construction*, published between 1930 and 1941, was conceived to propagate the spirit of the First Five-Year Plan, begun in 1928. Designed to promote a favorable image of

the USSR, it used photography and photomontage
to convey the virtues of the state and Stalin's rule.
The magazine was published in Russian, English,
German, French, and Spanish after 1938. Early issues
focused on state projects, some entirely devoted
to a single theme, like flight or mining. Collective
well-being was spotlighted as a viable means
of building economic health. Avant-garde designers
like Lissitzky, Rodchenko, Stepanova, Solomon
Telingater, and Nikolai Troshin, all connected
to Vkhutemas, were the principal designers, but
Lissitzky had the strongest influence. The magazine
exemplified how text, images, charts, and diagrams
could be integral components of the visual narrative.
Generally the typography did not conform to earlier
Constructivist formats pioneered by Lissitzky and
Rodchenko, but, from the outset, type was subordinate
to photographs and photomontage, which enabled
the designers to manipulate and transform otherwise
mundane imagery.

soviet typography

Avant-garde graphic designers saw their work as
a challenge to the old typographic order and as a
defining element to the new Soviet aesthetic.
Constructivist typography melded disparate typefaces in varying sizes (often within a single word) in
an unprecedented way; asymmetrical composition
became a defining trait of the modernist "New
Typography."[10] Yet there was arguably no official Soviet
typography. Type and, more frequently, hand-lettering
on posters and placards played only an incidental
role in the overall propaganda process.

Type invention was not a priority in the Soviet
Union. New typefaces were hard to come by, since
founding type was a costly process, and Cyrillic typefaces were not created in the rest of Europe. Soviet
graphic designers used preexisting typefaces rather
than create new designs. What is often called "Soviet

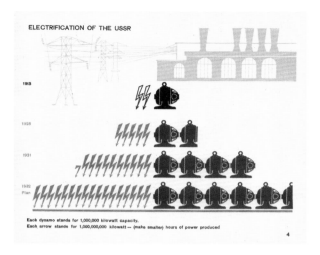

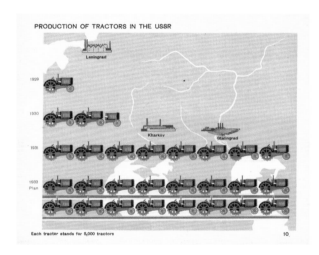

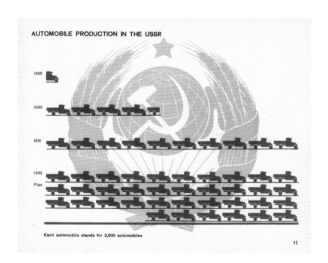

270–72. The struggle
for five years in four
This portfolio of modern
pictographs charts
the progress of Stalin's
First Five-Year Plan
in English.
c. 1934

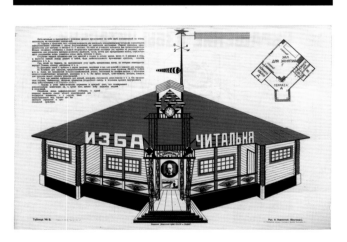

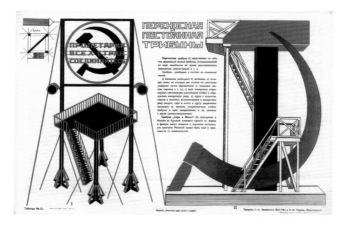

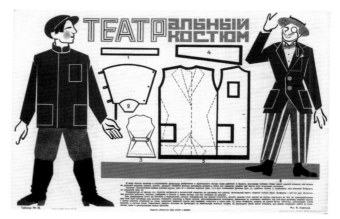

273–84. Art in everyday life: 36 pictures
This portfolio, designed and illustrated by I. Smirnov, provided young Communists with instructions on how to make a Soviet spectacle, from building a theater stage to designing costumes.
c. 1930

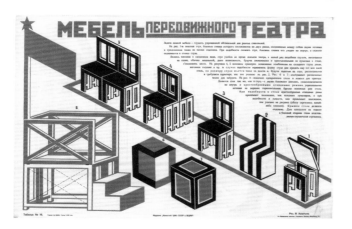

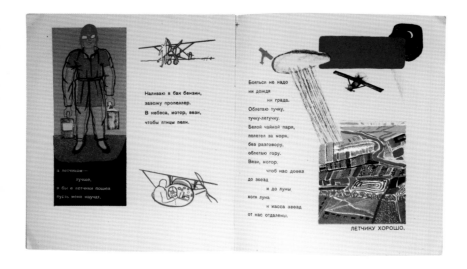

285–86. *Trip*
This book, illustrated by
Vladimir Mayakovsky,
tells of a journey through
the USSR.
1927

287–88. *Who to Be?*
Written by Mayakovsky
and illustrated by Nisson
Shifrin, this book depicts
what a young Soviet can
grow up to be.
1929

289–91. *Seven Wonders*
This book, written by
Samuil Marshak
with illustrations by
Mikhail Tsekhanovsky,
showcases the "wonders"
of the Soviet state.
1926

typography" refers not to specific new typefaces, but rather to a new look that reflected an aesthetic shift. Fonts were borrowed wherever they could be found to create unconventional typographic compositions. Lissitzky, Rodchenko, and Telingater, for example, combined serif and sans serif poster typefaces—metal and wood—to create architectonic letterforms. This Constructivist method of multiple type styles in variegated sizes defined a Soviet style that, though short-lived, had a lasting impact on designers outside the USSR.

Even after Socialist Realism became the dominant art form, no typeface came to be exclusively associated with the regime. And though no font was officially forbidden for being too bourgeois or reactionary, the elegant Romans and so-called perfume scripts common in European advertising were nowhere to be found in the stilted state-sanctioned Soviet graphic design. Type (even when printed in bright reds and yellows) became as nondescript and void of expression as all the art of the Stalinist era.

agitprop publishing for children

Children's books were an integral part of Soviet literacy campaigns, and were expertly written, illustrated, and designed in an effort to fight illiteracy.

As early as 1918 the newspaper *Pravda* (The truth), the official voice of the Russian Communist party, proclaimed, "The children's book as a major weapon for education must receive the widest possible distribution."[11] By 1924, two years after the Soviet Union was formed, the Central Committee announced its mission to develop a new kind of juvenile literature that would reject the bourgeois ornamentation that had dominated the *Mir iskusstva* (World of art) movement.[12] *Mir iskusstva* art, produced during the Silver Age (the eras of Alexander III and Nicholas II, from 1898 through the early 1920s), was the Russian counterpart to Art Nouveau, a curious fusion of

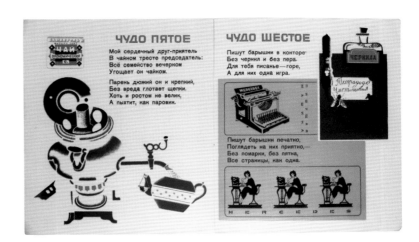

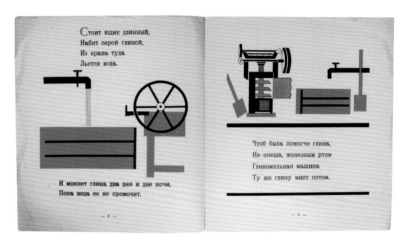

Japonisme, Pre-Raphaelite mannerisms, and Russian folk art.

After the 1917 October Revolution, with Russia in the throes of civil war, the Bolshevik state was bankrupt, forcing Lenin to reluctantly accept certain capitalistic measures. During this period of relative economic freedom, almost one hundred independent and state-run children's book publishers were founded in Moscow and Petrograd. High-quality books were produced with fine paper stock and advanced color technology. This attracted revolutionary artists—including Rodchenko, Klucis, Tatlin, Natan Altman, and El Lissitzky—to an art form that seemed to allow greater experimental liberty.

Where Do Dishes Come From? (1925) and *The Adventures of Charlie* (1924), both illustrated by Olga and Galena Chichagova, were rendered in a highly reductive style that was embraced by Communists because it was so diametrically opposed to the decorative excesses of the past. I. Sunderland's illustrations for Mayakovsky's *Strolling* (1926) also contain many of the abstract qualities that characterized Constructivist art. But reductive modernism was at its experimental zenith in Lissitzky's *Of Two Squares: A Suprematist Tale in Six Constructions*. The story of a black and a red square, the abstract children's book was published in Berlin in 1922 and shortly afterward in an issue of Theo van Doesburg's *De Stijl* magazine.

One of the most prolific artists was the Constructivist designer and illustrator Vladimir Lebedev, who illustrated over fifty books. Lebedev's mastery of abstract shapes, composition techniques, and propaganda graphics meant he knew how to convey a graphic message with ease. But more than other Constructivist image-makers, he was most able to soften his graphics, making them attractive to children. In a more traditional mode he would surround lush lithographed drawings of workers with bold red or black geometric type forms. And in a more abstract mode, he created his figures entirely out of the flat geometric shapes so prevalent at the time. His work exemplifies the communicative powers of Constructivism.

Lenin's wife, Nadezhda Krupskaya, a former schoolteacher, was personally committed to educating the masses and ending illiteracy. Working with Lunacharsky in the Commissariat of Enlightenment, Krupskaya helped establish free libraries and schools and lent her unflagging support to the production of a great number of picture books. The government supported such publications as agitprop, useful for spreading socialist ideals and Communist programs. Thousands of titles—from the seemingly benign *The Circus* to the decidedly propagandistic *How the Revolution Was Won*—were published in hefty quantities of ten to fifty thousand copies, and sometimes more.

But the golden age of socialism, and of children's book publishing,[13] ended in 1932, when Stalin collectivized the publishing industry. His functionaries decreed that artists and writers must embrace Socialist Realism's turgid "Red Romanticism" or pseudoclassicism. A copious number of children's books and pamphlets were produced during the initial surge of Stalin's artistic reform—when many proponents of the avant-garde were denounced as counterrevolutionaries—but books that failed to conform to sanctioned parameters were confiscated or destroyed. "Formalists," meaning those who experimented with abstract visual languages, were considered "enemies of the people." Anti-intellectualism reigned, in large part because of Leon Trotsky, who referred to the Formalist school as representing "abortive idealism." Such parochial thinking ultimately spilled over to children's books.

The politicization of children's books was a double-edged sword. Initially, children's books were a welcome new medium for revolutionary artists, but they ultimately became a prominent target of

292–94. *The Adventures of Charlie*
This book by Olga and Galena Chichagova was designed in the Productivist style with bold, simple graphics. 1927

295–97. *Where Do Dishes Come From?*
Illustrated by Olga and Galena Chichagova, this book was one in a series devoted to the manufacture of everyday objects. 1924

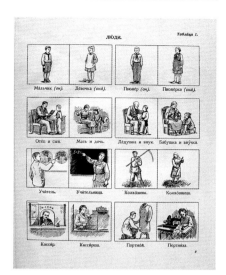

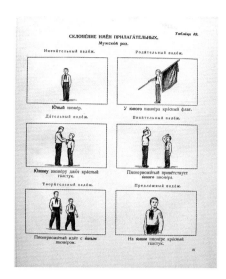

298–99. Children's postcards
Schoolchildren received postcards celebrating the virtues of being a Soviet Pioneer, with phrases like "The pioneer loves his motherland" and "The pioneer studies diligently and studiously."
c. 1955

300–302. Children's textbook
Illustrated textbook for young schoolchildren with explanations on how to be a good Soviet.
1959

Background:
A formation of young Soviet Pioneers at a summer camp in Novorossiysk in southern Russia.
1953

Stalinist repression. *Pravda* was clear about the official rhetoric when it announced in 1932, "Nowhere else does Formalism unmask itself to such a degree, as it does in drawings for children. It's precisely here that its inner emptiness, spiritual stagnation, and rottenness stick out with utmost strength."[14] Just as Suprematism and Constructivism were censured as too ambiguous to serve as tools of state propaganda, so the most progressive children's books were damned for not conveying unequivocal obedience to Stalin. As a result, the artists and authors of children's books— unless they agreed to conform—were prohibited from plying their craft, and some were even arrested and sent into exile.

the cult of personality

the lenin cult

Lenin was reluctant to promote himself. He was known to disdain adulation in favor of power. Nonetheless, as the prominent leader of the Bolshevik revolution, his friends and supporters tried to bestow upon him prophetic stature. Politburo member Grigory Zinoviev, one of Lenin's closest associates, proclaimed in 1919: "He is the authentic figure of a leader such as is born once in five hundred years."[15]

The first poster depicting Lenin in his characteristic ill-fitting suit, tie, and cap was published in 1918—the same year he survived an attempted assassination, which may have added some heroic glamour to his image. The most famous and most often reproduced of the official portraits, *Lenin on the Tribune* (1930), shows him surrounded by flags against the sky, light mystically shining behind him. Painted by Alexander Gerasimov, it served as a recruiting poster for the party. Lenin was depicted in a few classic poses. He was represented with his arm extended in a manner that suggested complete control over the masses, and in other staged poses—walking reflectively, speaking, listening to soldiers, pondering strategies and matters of state. Posters presented him as the ideologist, philosopher, and orator—alone mostly, but at times with other leaders. In contrast to stiff conventional heroic imagery, he was given a casual human quality—shown clutching his cap or casually slinging his coat over his arm. (Consistent with his ideal of a classless society, he wore civilian clothes rather than a military or political uniform). Most of the public images of the leader were paintings created from photographs. Lenin was not at all fond of sitting for portraits, and Nikolai Andreev, a realist painter and sculptor known for his 1905 portrait of Leo Tolstoy, was one of a very few selected to draw Lenin from life.

As Lenin's health declined, the appearance of his image increased (as did the dissemination of the images of those who sought to inherit his mantle). In homes and offices, photographs and paintings of Lenin filled nooks that were set up like the reliquaries where religious icons once had been kept: these were known as "Red Corners."

When Lenin died in January 1924, Stalin, who had been general secretary of the Communist party for two years, took advantage of the leadership vacuum, outwitting his rivals in the Politburo—Nikolai Bukharin, Grigory Zinoviev, Lev Kamenev, and Leon Trotsky—to position himself as the new leader. He was also a main instigator of the Lenin cult: Against Lenin's own wishes and those of his family, Stalin insisted that Lenin's body be embalmed and entombed in the brutish mausoleum designed by Alexei Shchusev and built in Red Square. Immediately after Lenin's death, Stalin prompted the Central Committee to issue directives on the production and distribution of busts, photographs, posters, banners, and all manner of public art that showed Lenin in official stances; he was

303. Lenin postcard
Engravings of Lenin by official, although often anonymous, artists graced many a souvenir postcard decades after he died, keeping the cult alive.
1966

Background:
Pedestrians pass by a huge portrait of Lenin on the facade of GUM department store in Moscow.
1967

also responsible for renaming Petrograd Leningrad. All sanctioned artwork except photography was controlled by the Committee for the Immortalization of Lenin's Memory, headed by chairman of the People's Commissars (or prime minister) Vyacheslav Molotov. For a brief time Lenin's image appeared on certain commercial products, including tobacco, but it was eventually deemed to diminish rather than enhance his stature.

Photographs and mechanical reproduction vastly increased the quantity of images available. Some were used as they were, without any reworking, while others found their way into Soviet revolutionary photomontages by Alexander Rodchenko, Gustav Klucis, and other avant-garde artists.

With its radically manipulated form, montage was a perfectly compliant tool. Although they were rarely photographed together, Stalin was cut and pasted into photographs with Lenin to give the illusion that they were close friends and political peers. Even as the Lenin cult developed, Stalin presented himself alongside Lenin in posters, banners, and

С ПРАЗДНИКОМ
ВЕЛИКОГО ОКТЯБРЯ!

304–8. Lenin at work
Lenin at a memorial to
Karl Marx and Friedrich
Engels in Moscow,
1918 (304); reading
Pravda in 1918 (305);
with his wife in the town
of Kashimo in 1920
(306); speaking against
anti-Jewish pogroms
for a gramophone
recording in 1919 (307);
posing in the courtyard
of the Kremlin in 1919
(308).

309. Waving Lenin
This official portrait
of Lenin waving to the
masses, wearing his
famous *kepochka*, "little
hat," and revolutionary
red ribbon, was taken
in 1920 and appeared
on the first page of most
textbooks. This postcard
was printed in 1967.

310. Triumphant return
This painting by Mikhail Sokolov shows Lenin arriving at the Finland Railway Station in Petrograd in April 1917 after his years in exile. Pictured just behind him is Joseph Stalin, who was not present at this historic event.
c. 1934

311. Lenin in hiding
This drawing depicts Lenin in hiding during the political turmoil in the months leading up to the Bolshevik revolution.
c. 1930

312. Stalin meets Lenin
Painting by I. Vepkhvadze of Lenin and Stalin's mythic first meeting at a 1905 conference in Tammerfors, Finland.
c. 1930

badges. While Lenin was the undisputed father of the revolution, Stalin positioned himself to become the Big Brother. Along with Marx and Engels, Lenin and Stalin were frequently emblazoned on the endless array of seals and banners produced by party and state. By the end of the decade, Stalin was omnipresent. In 1947 John Steinbeck visited the Soviet Union and wrote in his diary, "Everything in the Soviet Union takes place under the fixed stare of the plaster, bronze, drawn or embroidered eye of Stalin. His portrait does not just hang in every museum but in a museum's every room."[16]

the stalin cult

Lenin sought to maintain a modest profile; Stalin wanted just the opposite—though he, too, purported to be modest. The promotion of Lenin's image over Stalin's own was a short-lived ruse that ended once he was able to acquire power for himself. Stalin saw in art only a utilitarian purpose, which was to bolster the image of the leader. Soviet functionaries falsified art and photographs by skillfully retouching out purged leaders and bureaucrats, and by changing signs and banners to point more directly to ideological needs.[17] The airbrush was one of Stalin's most effective propaganda weapons.

The Stalin cult established him as the "Great Leader and Teacher of the Soviet People" and "Chief Architect and Builder of Our Socialist Motherland"; other hyperbolic honorifics were lavished upon him as well. In photographs and paintings he was pictured as a friend of the common people and of children, too. Blemishes were eradicated—Stalin suffered terribly from psoriasis over most of his body and had a withered arm; here again, the airbrush was a good ally.

The earliest paintings and posters of Stalin presented him in close proximity to Lenin, the compositions manipulated to make them appear

313. Dubious meeting
Most historians agree that Stalin was montaged into this photograph of Lenin in Gorki. The meeting probably never happened.
1922

314. Stalin and Lenin
This montaged photograph includes Stalin with key members of the Central Committee—Vyacheslav Molotov, Anastas Mikoyan, Kliment Voroshilov, Georgi Dimitrov—next to Lenin's embalmed body.
1924

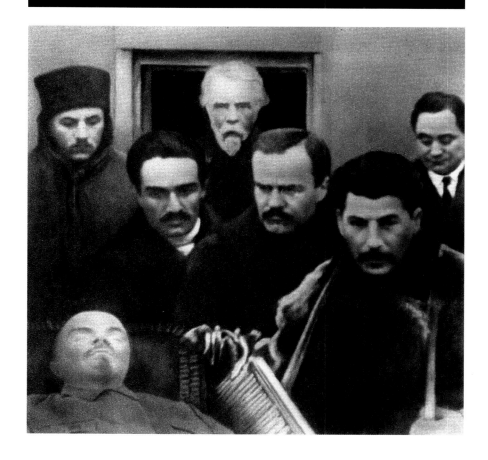

closer than they were in real life. Subsequent images positioned Stalin in front of busts or statues of Lenin, suggesting the former's ascension. Books recounted Stalin's youth, and visual hagiographies were sold as souvenirs and postcards.

Stalin's portraits can be categorized according to the following archetypes: the ideologue (shown presiding over Soviet congresses); the progressive (seen at electrical plants, factories, and other public works); the friend of the people (shaking hands with the masses); and the military hero (in formal uniform and usually in profile, or with his head slightly turned). They were reproduced on everyday materials—from booklets and brochures, stamps and seals, to diplomas and certificates. Ubiquitous in plaster, bronze, ink, or paint, Stalin's image was in every bus or train station, in every office building, and in all parks and public spaces. The leader's presence—all-seeing and all-hearing—was felt everywhere.

After the great purges of the 1930s—orchestrated by Stalin to expunge all opposition to his reign,

including leading figures in the Communist party and the military—Stalin's image began to change. More emphasis was placed on his omnipotence than on his amicability. Stalin's favored painter, Alexander Gerasimov, portrayed him in monumental stance with an intensive gaze.

After World War II, Stalin added military victory to his claimed accomplishments, and his graphic deification was complete. No longer presented in the company of others (even Lenin), he stood alone, superior to party and state. In the postwar years, his shock of black hair grayed, and he was represented in more stately poses. Stalin's three-quarter portrait by S. N. Melamud and P. D. Getman became the most common representation used in the Soviet Union and by other Communist countries.

Stalin was one of the most adulated of twentieth-century tyrants and, despite the atrocities committed under his rule, his image remained intact until his death from a massive stroke in 1953. It was Nikita Khrushchev, first secretary of the Communist party

315–17. Stalin
Official portrait,
c. 1930 (315); portrait
featured in *Soviet
Almanac*, 1947 (316);
official portrait at desk,
date unknown (317).

318. Generalissimo
Stalin
The highest Soviet
military rank was
created for Stalin in
the wake of his
victory in World War II.
This portrait was
realized by Irakly
Toidze, a well-known
official Soviet artist.
27 June 1945

319. **319. Diploma**
Stalin's image features
prominently on this
citation for wartime
service.
1945

320. Victory vase
This very large vase
with a portrait by
Alexei Skvortsov was
presented to Stalin
on the first anniversary
of the victory over
the Nazis.
1946

321–22. English books
The Stalin Pocket
Library series (321),
and International
Publishers, in New
York (322), published
Soviet material
in the United States.
1930, 1935

323. *Review*
The cover of this publi-
cation by the Young
Communist League of
New York was designed
by the American
Phil Stern. It features
a painting by Irakly
Toidze showing Stalin
with local men at
a hydroelectric power
plant in Georgia.
1939

Background:
Cheering Communist
youths lead a procession
with a large portrait
of Stalin.
Date unknown

from 1953 to 1964, who famously dismantled Stalin's
cult of personality at the twentieth Party Congress
in 1956. The "secret speech" delivered in a closed
session of the congress and later leaked to party
activists and local party meetings meted out harsh
criticism of Stalin's show trials, purges, and gulag
system. At the same time, Khrushchev reinstated
Lenin alongside Marx as the visage of the Soviet
Union. As a symbol of his fall from grace, Stalin's
body was moved from his place in Lenin's mausoleum
on Red Square to a burial spot along the Kremlin
wall. Although Mikhail Gorbachev's policies of
glasnost and perestroika were still two decades away,
what became known as the "Khrushchev thaw"
relaxed censorship and sparked a relative artistic
liberalization.

321

322

323

THE 16TH PARTY CONGRESS
J. STALIN

JOSEPH STALIN
THE SOVIETS AND THE INDIVIDUAL
INTERNATIONAL PUBLISHERS
2c

REVIEW
December, 1939   10 cents

socialist realism

Lenin personally abhorred abstraction and disliked all the modern genres. He did not wage war against the avant-garde, however, but he believed that realism achieved the greatest outreach to the masses. If Lenin had sympathies for any art movement, it was the group of realists known as the Itinerants, whose name derived from the touring exhibitions they circulated around Russia. Focused on criticizing czarist society and the bourgeoisie, the Itinerants followed Lenin's vision of art's "total submission to the party." They produced realistic paintings that reflected the class struggle in Russia. The Itinerants' highly detailed work became a model for later Socialist Realism.

Lenin also approved of monumentalism— a genre essentially similar to the imperial styles and religious iconography of earlier eras in Russia. In 1918 he published his *Plan for Monumental Propaganda*, a blueprint for the construction of public monuments to the worker, peasant, and revolutionary leaders. Each monument was to be designed for utmost visual impact on the landscape and produced in the realist style.

This conservative approach became the hallmark of the most influential visual and graphic arts group in the Soviet Union, the Association of Artists of Revolutionary Russia, formed in 1922. The association was faithful to *partiinost* (party-mindedness) and called their revolutionary style "Heroic Realism." Their manifesto stated, "We will depict the present day:

the life of the Red Army, the workers, the peasants, the revolutionaries, and the heroes of labor."[18] The goal of these realists was to depict the "New Soviet Person"— athlete, worker, and peasant: the embodiment of efficiency. By the time of Lenin's death in 1924, the association had built the solid foundation on which Socialist Realism would be based.

Socialist Realism (not to be confused with the Western concept of "social realism," in which topical events are depicted to critique and illuminate social issues) was the theme of the First Congress of Soviet Writers in 1934. At the time the term did not refer to a specific style but was summed up in slogans like "Workers of the World Unite," "All Power to the Soviets," and "Peace, Land, and Bread," which provided simple, clean helpings of ideological wisdom to the masses. The object of Socialist Realism was to romanticize and heroicize the state, its leaders, and its instruments (such as the Red Army).

The *Great Soviet Encyclopedia* credits Stalin as having originated the term *Socialist Realism*, but it first appeared in an article in the May 1932 *Literary Gazette*, which stated, "The masses demand an artist's honesty, truthfulness, and a revolutionary socialist realism in the representation of the proletarian revolution."[19]

By 1934 Maxim Gorky called for the adoption of Socialist Realism as the true Soviet method. He proclaimed:

324. *Lenin's Send-off to the Red Troops Leaving Moscow for the Polish Front* This painting by Isaak Brodsky, created before Socialist Realism became an official movement, was one of the famous examples of the style. 1920

Background: May Day celebration in Moscow. 1 May 1951

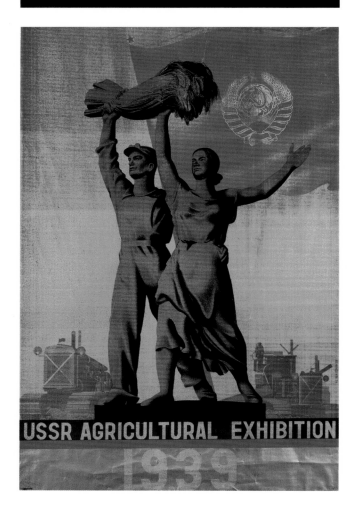

Socialist Realism firmly supports the view of existence as action, as a creation whose aim is the continual development of the most precious individual capabilities of man to ensure victory over the forces of nature, his health and long life, the great happiness of being able to live on this earth, which in answer to his ever-increasing needs he wishes to make over entirely, into a magnificent home for all mankind united in a single family.... Socialist Realism [is] the realism of men who transform and rebuild the world.[20]

Like Lenin, Stalin did not pretend to be an artist, but he was by all evidence a cultural dictator, who maintained total control over Soviet art and design. He was hailed by one acolyte for his "words of genius about Soviet art as an art of Socialist Realism, representing the peak of all the progressive strivings of the aesthetic thought of mankind."[21] Stalin managed to conflate Lenin's art ideal with characteristics of *narodnost* (social responsibility), *ideinost* (ideological content), and *klassovost* (class consciousness). Socialist Realism became the official literary style in 1932, when Stalin issued his decree "On the Reconstruction of Literary and Art Organizations," but he never gave concrete guidelines for a visual Socialist Realism. His personal taste, like Lenin's, tended toward realism in the style of the Itinerants, and he encouraged artists to elaborate on these general ideas.

Socialist Realism prescribed form and content. Its alleged goals were historical accuracy in depicting the revolutionary development of the party and state, and to make art that would contribute to the

327

328

329. *A Political
Demonstration by
the Workers of Batum
Under the leadership
of Comrade Stalin
in 1902*
This painting by
Apollon Kutateladze
was included in the
1939 exhibition "Stalin
and the Soviet People."
c. 1939

330. *Lenin on the Tribune*
This famous painting
by Alexander Gerasimov
is a potent example
of Socialist Realism.
1930

331. Heroic Stalin
This painting portrays
Stalin standing in
full military uniform
in his Kremlin office.
c. 1935

332. *Worker and
Collective Farm Woman*
This steel sculpture
by Vera Mukhina was
originally displayed
at the 1937 World's
Fair in Paris and
was installed at the
northern entrance to the
All-Russia Exhibition
Center in 1939. Mukhina
received one of the
first Stalin prizes for
the sculpture in 1941.
1937

ideological transformation and education of workers in the spirit of socialism. Despite the antiromanticism inherent in the Itinerants' realism, another style, "revolutionary romanticism," an idealization of the worker and soldier—and leader—emerged from the burgeoning Socialist Realist style.

As the official Soviet style, Socialist Realism reduced art to slavish compliance to the state. Avant-garde art was eradicated. Ultimately, even the few glimmers of novelty in the Socialist Realist style were destroyed as Stalin's vicious purges—the Great Terror—reached a fevered pitch in the 1930s.

МОЛОДЫЕ СТРОИТЕЛИ КОММУНИЗМА!
ВПЕРЁД, К НОВЫМ УСПЕХАМ В ТРУДЕ И УЧЁБЕ!

333. Glory to those who defend our country! This heroic poster is typical of Socialist Realism. 1948

334. Glory to the great october! The symbols of the USSR, including the *Aurora* battleship that sounded the signal to storm the Winter Palace in 1917, are represented in this poster. c. 1966

335. Young builders of Communism! Go forward to the new successes in labor and study! The young man in Mikhail Soloviev's Socialist Realist poster holds a book titled *Lenin–Stalin*. 1949

ПОД ЗНАМЕНЕМ
МАРКСИЗМА-ЛЕНИНИЗМА,
ПОД РУКОВОДСТВОМ
КОММУНИСТИЧЕСКОЙ
ПАРТИИ-
ВПЕРЕД,
К ПОБЕДЕ

336

С праздником
Великой
Октябрьской
социалистической
революции!

the "new openness"

Though the Soviet government maintained strict control over art and design, the emphasis on Socialist Realism was tempered in the wake of Nikita Khrushchev's denunciation of Stalin's crimes in 1956. The situation began to loosen. *Samizdat*, clandestine copies of government-suppressed literature, were widely distributed and became a vehicle for literary and artistic expression. Though design advances were slow to take effect, Western techniques, from typography to layout, were gradually introduced. Ministries involved with export began using the typeface Helvetica in their promotion materials, and a small market for modern type fonts allowed designers to look at Western models.

By the early 1970s, advertising was being introduced in the Soviet Union. The Union of Trade Advertising published *Reklame* (Advertising), which surveyed the work of advertising groups throughout the USSR. Since the Baltic republics had slightly more exposure to Western media, their advertising was more advanced than that being produced in Moscow and Leningrad.

By the mid 1970s a young generation of Soviet graphic artists hungered for inspiration. Paradoxically, Western design was easier to come by than works by the Russian avant-garde. The Swiss design magazine *Graphis*, which featured design from the Western and Eastern blocs, was distributed like a *samizdat* publication. Designers did not simply copy these Western models, but analyzed what was good, and then fashioned their own styles. Much of this was done in secret and shown only in private exhibits. The Soviet Artists Union, a monolithic organization that controlled all fine and applied arts, obstructed the emergence of new ideas. Shifts in Soviet style were cautiously tentative.

Under Leonid Brezhnev, party leader from 1964 to 1982, Communist visual culture did not progress. But Mikhail Gorbachev's policies of glasnost and perestroika ushered in a cultural revival in the Soviet Union. Although printed on flimsy paper, glasnost posters expressed the frustrations of a nation long under Communist oppression. They addressed unmentioned social ills, including compassion for the handicapped, drug and alcohol addiction, prostitution, and AIDS. Governmental abuses, the bloated bureaucracy, and residual Stalinism were subjects of criticism. This was truly a new openness. And though perestroika posters lacked some of the spontaneity and mobilizing force of Bolshevik posters of the 1920s, when compared to numbing Socialist Realism they were revolutionary.

336. The great October socialist revolution! After Stalin's demise, his image was replaced by those of Karl Marx and Lenin. 1966

Background: Military parade in Moscow on May Day. 1 May 1956

the communist chinese

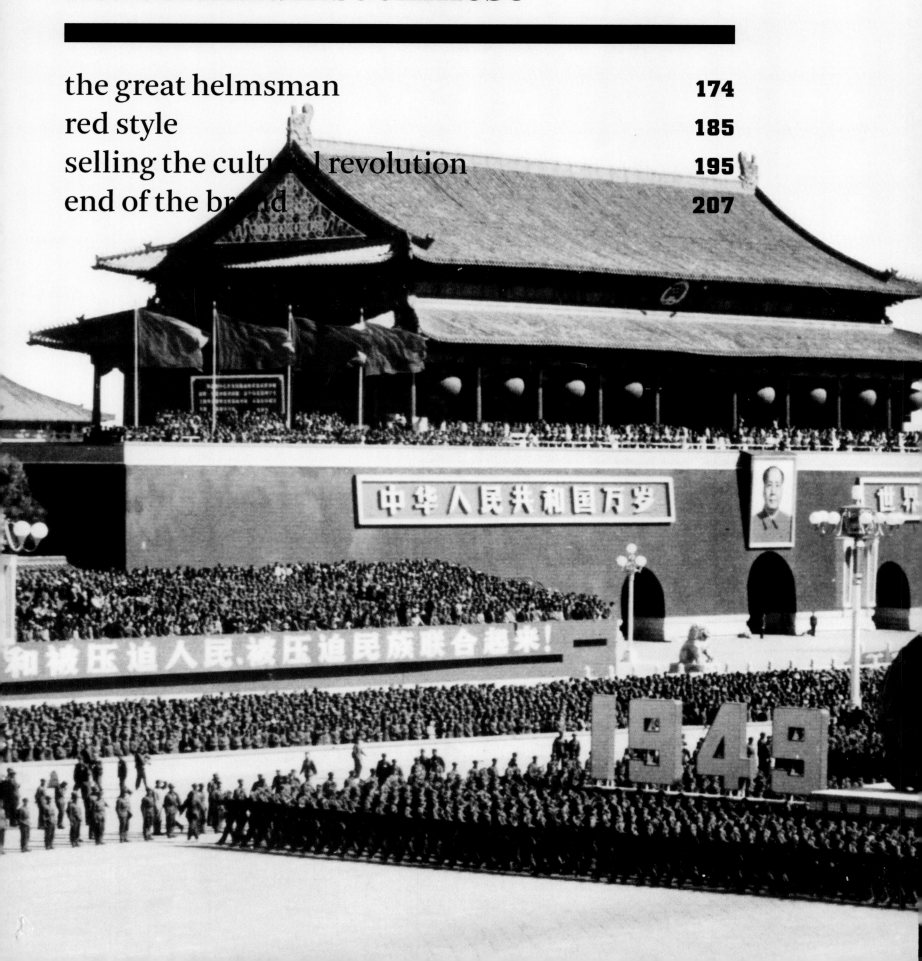

大团结万岁

伟大的中国共产党万岁

庆祝伟大的中华人民共和国成立二十周年

1969

the great helmsman

This meeting is called today for the purpose of making literature and art faithfully perform the functions of a component part of the entire mechanism of the Revolution, so that they may become powerful weapons uniting the people together, educating the people, and dealing blows against the enemy.
—Mao Zedong, 1941

mao as trademark

On 18 August 1966, hordes of Chinese youth, wearing red armbands and waving Mao Zedong's Little Red Book, converged on Beijing's Tiananmen Square. These young revolutionaries had come not to fight against the authority of the Communist establishment but to celebrate Mao's resurgence. Mao had devised an alliance with Chinese youth to regain power within the Central Committee. His plan was to goad the youthful masses into a generational conflict to uproot the influence of other Communist leaders and, with the unconditional allegiance of an entire generation, reclaim power for himself. In a well-orchestrated symbolic gesture, Song Binbin presented the seventy-three-year-old leader with a revolutionary armband. The Red Guard armband became a trait as familiar in official portraits and photographs of Mao as the mole on his face.

Mao was the revolutionary hero of the Long March, who had defeated the capitalist forces of the Kuomintang and established the People's Republic of China in 1949. Though he still enjoyed great prestige as a revolutionary hero around the country, by the mid-1960s his power within the Chinese Communist party had seriously eroded. Although he retained the party chairmanship, he had been persuaded to resign his post as head of state. Mao's Great Leap Forward (his Second Five-Year Plan, proclaimed in 1958) had been a tragic failure. The Chinese had hoped to transform the agricultural and industrial sectors of the economy through collectivization by focusing on manpower rather than on mechanization. The diversion of farm labor to small-scale industry created an agricultural crisis; bureaucratic incompetence, combined with natural disasters, resulted in one of the most tragic human catastrophes of the twentieth century. After the communal farm system broke down and famine took the lives of millions of peasants, Mao reluctantly stepped aside and became the "dead ancestor," as he referred to himself in his imposed semiretirement. The baton was passed to the opposing faction in the Communist party, those who believed that economic incentive and private property were essential to rescuing China's economy.

The Cultural Revolution was triggered by Mao's regret that he had relinquished power so easily. By mobilizing high school and college students to "bombard the headquarters"[1]—to attack party structures and traditional figures of authority— he gained the support of an entire generation. What followed were the ten cataclysmic years of the Great Proletarian Cultural Revolution, which wreaked havoc on Chinese society until Mao's death in 1976.

Chairman Mao, the "most venerable leader and greatest revolutionary instructor," as the Red Guards referred to him, ignited political fervor with slogans such as "Revolution is not a crime" and "It is right to rebel." Aggressively supported by opportunistic army

337. Great leader chairman Mao
This official portrait of Mao by Zhang Zhenshi has been called the Chinese *Mona Lisa*. 1950

338. Mao saluting the Red Guard
This portrait, painted on glass, was based on a photograph of Mao reviewing the Red Guard from Tiananmen Gate. 1967

339. Paper cut
Mao's likeness might be emblazoned on anything, using any medium. This image was produced using the traditional Chinese paper-cutting technique. c. 1967

Background:
Workers march in Beijing holding *dazibao* (big-character posters) and the official portrait of Mao by Zhang Zhenshi. 1968

Previous spread:
Red Guards celebrate the national holiday in Beijing. 1 October 1966

340. Radiant Mao
This folio cover
shows Mao in People's
Liberation Army (PLA)
uniform as if in front
of a radiant sun.
c. 1974

341. Loyalty
This woodcut of Mao,
which celebrates the
chairman's longevity,
compares him to
the morning sun and
the Chinese people
to sunflowers.
1968

**342. Our work will
succeed**
Mao's profile is juxta-
posed against images of
loyal citizens—worker,
peasant, soldier, athlete,
and Red Guard.
c. 1968

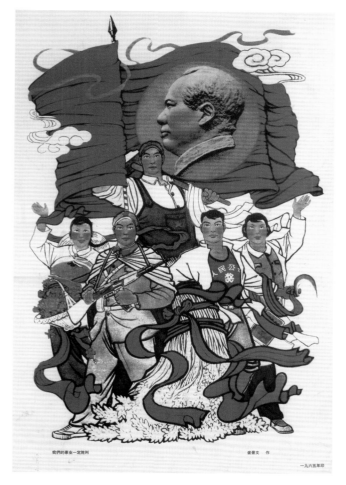

generals and scheming sycophants, the Cultural Revolution targeted the cultural elite as well as party moderates, and called into action a militant force whose loyalties were captured through intensive propaganda.

Mao's visage was painted by many different "art workers" and is believed to be one of the most widely reproduced faces in the world. Mao images were hung in public spaces, schools, offices, and homes; failure to display them would result in severe recriminations. His most famous portrait, painted by Zhang Zhenshi in 1950, gives the impression that the chairman's flesh radiates light, and is sometimes referred to as China's *Mona Lisa*, owing to the inscrutable hint of a smile. Mao was shown in countless poses—smiling or stern, at different ages, and wearing different uniforms. To maintain

the illusion of proximity to the people, he never wore medals or other distinctive badges or regalia. He was often portrayed as a friendly "trade character," in contemporary advertising argot. His cheery mien—smiling gently, sometimes laughing—called to mind a sweet father figure rather than an iron-fisted Big Brother.

the little red book

Mao's uniform resulted in a unique fashion trend. The *zhongshan* suit (known in the West as the Mao jacket) replicated the typical uniform worn during the war against the Japanese. A reminder of Mao's heroic past, it was worn by the Red Guards in a sign of allegiance. But the most popular object to come out of the Cultural Revolution was *Quotations from*

343

344

QUOTATIONS FROM
CHAIRMAN
MAO TSE-TUNG

345

346

347

348

343–48. Mao books
Lin Biao compiled Mao's quotations into what was commonly referred to as the "Little Red Book," but also known as *Highest Commands* and *Mao Zedong Thought*. Slogans such as "Read Chairman Mao's books, listen to Chairman Mao's words, follow Chairman Mao's direction" and "Forever loyal to Chairman Mao" were printed on the covers (343–45). The Foreign Languages Press produced the book for export in 1968 (344). Notebooks used by the Red Guards to jot down the Chairman's lessons also prominently featured Mao's face and sayings (346–48). 1966–77

349. Reading Mao
Workers in Qinghai Province read the works of Mao. The placards read, "Hurray Chairman Mao" and "Hurray Chinese Communism." 1967

Background:
A convoy carrying Chairman Mao passes a crowd of Red Guards brandishing Little Red Books on Tiananmen Square in Beijing. 1966

Chairman Mao Zedong, the "Little Red Book" initially published in 1964 and compiled by Mao's heir apparent, Lin Biao. Uniformly covered in red plastic— a protective material often used in Chinese book publishing—this revolutionary bible includes 427 quotations, divided thematically into thirty-three chapters. The quotations, which range in length from a sentence to a few short paragraphs, draw heavily on about two dozen documents originally published in the four volumes of Mao's *Selected Works*, published in mass quantities two years later, in 1966. Lin Biao ordered members of the People's Liberation Army to read the Little Red Book every day, and the Red Guards carried copies of it in small red pouches hung around

their necks, or in "Serve the People" shoulder bags. The book was printed in millions of copies, produced by the army, different Red Guard committees, and several political departments, each of which gave the book a slightly different title, such as *Chairman Mao's Highest Commands* and *Mao Zedong Thought*, often including a quotation as subtitle—"Long life and success to Mao Zedong Thought" or the curiously phrased "Pay respect to and learn from the Red Flag Rubber Company Mao Zedong Propaganda Team."

Quotations from Chairman Mao Zedong is now universally known as the Little Red Book, and its binding and format have achieved a fame that surpasses its content.

全世界人民团结起来，打倒美帝！打倒苏修！打倒各国反动派！

无产阶级文化大革命，实质上是在社会主义条件下，无产阶级反对资产阶级和一切剥削阶级的政治大革命，是中国共产党及其领导下的广大革命人民群众和国民党反动派长期斗争的继续，是无产阶级和资产阶级阶级斗争的继续。

伟大领袖毛主席万岁
世界人民大团结万岁

mao badges

Mao pins and badges, which had first appeared in China before the formation of the People's Republic but were produced only sporadically until the mid-1960s, were hugely popular during the Cultural Revolution. Before 1966, Mao badges were made at the state-owned Beijing Red Flag Badge Factory and Shanghai United Badge and Insignia Factory. As the vortex of leftist radicals at the start of the Cultural Revolution, Shanghai produced the first new Mao badges in mid-July 1966. Initially the numbers were limited, but by August they were up to 175,000, and by September production had reached 1.3 million. Lin Biao, who served as Mao's de facto image consultant, made certain that the flood of Mao badges coincided with a mid-August propaganda campaign, which aimed to get a copy of the *Selected Works of Chairman Mao* into the hands of every citizen.

Collecting Mao badges soon developed into a frenzy. Cheap to produce in thin metal, they were made in vast quantities; badge factories and army units across the country stamped out several billion badges in thousands of iterations. Those produced by Red Guard units featured Mao's profile against a red or blue background. On the back were engraved a few words on the nature of the celebration. These pins were an integral part of the cult of Mao; over ninety percent of Chinese wore Mao badges.

Designed by Red Guard "art workers," the badges evolved in essentially three phases. During the first phase, lasting from July 1966 to May 1967, most of the badges were small, round, and tin. In the second stage, from around May 1967 to fall 1968, the badges were more ornate and featured details of specific events. The final stage of badge production lasted from fall 1968 to winter 1969, when all of China's provinces and autonomous regions officially came under the control of Cultural Revolution committees—a time, as the Chinese described it, when "the whole country was awash in red." The types

350. Anti-imperialism
This poster, with the inscription "All people of the world unite to overthrow *American imperialism*, to overthrow *Soviet revisionism*, to overthrow *reactionaries* from all nations," (words in italics reflect those written in black on the poster) denounces the Soviet Union in a period of strained Sino-Soviet relations.
1969

351. Celebrating the establishment of the Hunan Cultural Revolution Committee
This poster, which shows Lin Biao, Zhou Enlai, Chen Boda, Kang Sheng, and Jiang Qing (Madame Mao), marching alongside Mao in Tiananmen Square, is a rare surviving example. Lin, Chen, Kang, and Jiang were later deemed to be traitors to the country, and all images showing them close to Mao were destroyed.
1968

352. Solidarity with the Third World
This poster shows Mao and Lin Biao marching with people from Third World nations.
1967

353–58. Mao buttons and plaques
Typical early tin buttons from 1966 (353–54); metal plaques from 1969–70 (355–56); porcelain buttons with young Mao in Yan'an at the end of the Long March in 1936 (357) and older Mao (358), both c. 1966.

359–60. *Zhi-bu Sheng-huo* (Party life) This illustrated weekly magazine published official stories of the Communist party. 1965–66

361–62. Postage stamps Chinese stamps were ostensibly mini-posters, portraying Mao in various iterations as well as scenes glorifying Communist Chinese life. 1966–76

Background: Residents of Shanghai celebrate the founding of the People's Republic of China with a large poster of Mao (right) and Zhu De, leader of the People's Liberation Army. 1949

of materials used increased greatly, as did the sizes and shapes of the badges. Mao's profile was framed by various scenes and with numerous slogans. Badge production reached its zenith in April and May of 1969, in concert with the opening on 1 April of the Ninth Congress of the Chinese Communist Party.

Mao badges played a role in the People's Republic foreign policy. To spread the Mao gospel, they were exported to Third World countries along with Little Red Books, and Communist party members were ordered to give Mao badges to foreign guests.

Production was summarily restricted when, on 12 June 1969, the Central Committee issued a circular with the heading "Several issues to pay attention to when disseminating images of Chairman Mao."[2] It declared, "Unless approved by the Party Center, it is no longer permissible to manufacture Chairman Mao badges." One explanation was

that precious materials crucial for China's industrial production were being consumed by the badges. Another reason for the discontinuation may have been Mao's increasing distrust of Lin Biao, who was behind the badge mania.[3]

361

362

363

364

red style

proletarian art or content over form

The greatest volume of imagery immediately recognized as Communist Chinese propaganda was produced during the Cultural Revolution, but key decisions regarding art and design were made as early as 1941, years prior to the founding of the People's Republic of China (PRC).

Until the creation of the PRC, the Chinese Communists used a simple red banner—the color established by the Soviet Union as the hue of international Communism. The flag of the People's Republic, first hoisted in 1949, is red with five yellow stars. The large one represents the Communist party's overarching power, while the four small ones stand for the workers, peasants, petit bourgeoisie, and patriotic capitalists.[4]

Mao presented his view of the role of artists and writers at the famous 1942 Yan'an Forum on Literature and Art: "Works of literature and art, as ideological forms, are products of the reflection in the human brain of the life of a given society. Revolutionary literature and art are the products of reflection of the life of the people in the brains of revolutionary writers and artists."[5]

Mao elaborated on these ideas. He claimed that cultural manifestations should be designed for workers, peasants, and soldiers—that is, the proletariat. It was considered the artist's job to become acquainted with the lives of the proletariat, and to toil among them to gain knowledge of their circumstances.

Mao dictated that art also elevate the status of the proletariat. In a 1955 pamphlet that analyzed the Chinese art program, Communist critic Zhong Zhao explained that a person born under the Communist regime would thus be "content to become a worker, or a peasant or a member of the armed forces."[6] Mao instructed culture cadres to practice literary and art criticism, to draw out the political nature of artworks. He said, "All dark forces jeopardizing the safety of the masses must be relentlessly exposed; whereas all the revolutionary struggles of the masses must be praised and applauded."[7]

In 1943, when the Ministry of Publicity of China's Central Political Bureau issued a copy of Mao's Yan'an speech, his words were considered law. In 1949, when the Communists established their government in Beijing, they adopted what amounted to a constitution, the "Common Program of the Chinese People's Political Consultative Conference." Its article 15, chapter 5, outlined the "Cultural and Educational Policy," which stated: "Art shall be promoted to serve the people, to awaken their political consciousness, and to enhance their enthusiasm for labor." Art would be targeted at specific constituencies: workers, for example, would be shown machines and plants; peasants, collectivized farms; and soldiers, airplanes and weaponry.

363. *Collection of Revolutionary Songs*
The ubiquitous and iconic red flag heralds this revolutionary anthology.
Date unknown

364. The proletarian revolution faction has seized power!
This woodcut is a typical example of cheaply produced Red Guard posters.
1968

Background:
Members of the People's Liberation Army raise their fists in the Communist salute.
1967

『經中國人民郵政登記認爲第一類新聞紙
類北京郵政管理局登記執照第七十九號』

為祖國獻出一切
Отдадим все для родины

北京：工人出版社發行
上海：徐勝記印刷廠承印
Рабочее издательство:
Пекин.

365. Give everything for your country
This poster was published in the *Chinese Workers' Pictorial,* the journal of the All-Chinese Federation of Labor, which was aimed at readers in the Soviet Union. 1950

366. Long March poster
This poster, using the traditional Chinese paper-cutting technique, commemorates the Long March with the famous image of Mao in Yan'an in 1936. 1972

367. Autumn Harvest Uprising
This paper cut celebrates the Mao-led peasant insurrection against the Kuomintang in 1927. Although the uprising failed, Mao continued to work in rural areas, establishing peasant soviets. 1972

In 1953, over a decade after Mao's Yan'an speech, the Chinese Communists convened the Second Conference of Writers and Artists, at which a call was made to "popularize" art. The Communists argued that if art was not popularized—or "universal" in the Communist sense of a borderless, classless society— it would lose its propaganda value. Interestingly, Mao voiced the concern that this could cause art to become bland or mediocre—the fundamental peril of making art subservient to politics. But ultimately Mao concluded that artists "naturally must obey the political wishes of the class and Party and subject themselves to the revolutionary duties of the definite revolutionary period."[8] This meant, practically speaking, that art was to praise the "exalted character" of Chinese leaders and of the People's Liberation Army, as well as land reform; furthermore, it was to decry counterrevolutionary elements and declared enemies of the Communists.

In 1954 the First National People's Congress, the Chinese legislative body, adopted an official state constitution, and the first administrative bodies of art and culture were created. The Ministry of Publicity of the Central Political Bureau, directed by Lu Tingyi, established the Ministry of Cultural Affairs, which sanctioned artists and governed the production of art. The ministry maintained satellite bureaus of culture in the provinces, which monitored cinema as well as art. Ideological purity was valued above all else. For a decade after the founding of the People's Republic, some traditional art themes were accepted— landscapes, birds, and flowers among them—but by the early 1960s traditional techniques such as brush painting and woodcut were being rejected in favor of Soviet-inspired Socialist Realist painting. Adoption of the Stalinist style was a deliberate effort to produce art that would serve the needs of socialism. The People's Liberation Army contributed to the new style: Much of the content of the new art was drawn from noble qualities and heroic deeds of soldiers and was often

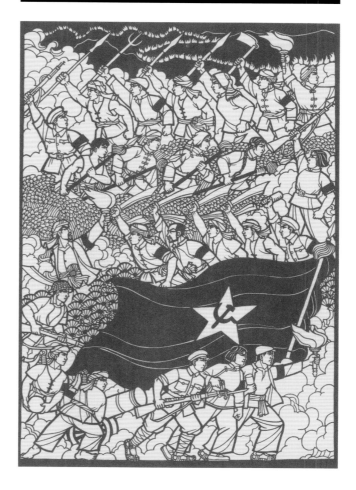

368–75. *Zhi-bu Sheng-huo* (Party life) This official weekly magazine was printed on cheap, porous paper with color covers and black-and-white interior pages. The heavily illustrated stories extolled industrial, military, and agricultural achievements. 1960–66

376

热爱劳动 REAI LAODONG

377

杨家岭的早晨

378

地雷战

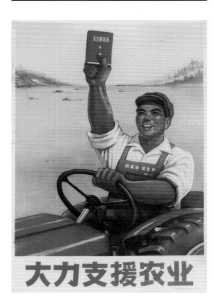

379

380

大力支援农业

381

提高文化,向现代化、正规化国防军前进!

376–81. Poster propaganda
'Love Labor Work' calls young Communists to work with gusto (376); 'Mao plants' shows Mao watering seedlings, probably a reference to his tree planting campaign in the early 1950s (377); 'Landmine battle' shows militia how to fight a guerilla war (378); this poster appears to show a celebratory meeting of Mao with peasants holding red flags with the hammer and sickle, perhaps in reference to the 1927 Autumn Harvest Uprising (379); 'Strongly support agriculture' and 'Modernize our knowledge: national defense moves forward' feature Mao's Little Red Book prominently (380–81).
1967–70

382. Welcome to the National Science Conference
Socialist Realism takes a turn toward kitsch in this painting promoting science in the People's Republic.
c. 1980

produced by the soldiers themselves. Scenes of great revolutionary moments or idealized portraits of heroes were generally painted on canvas and then reproduced in multiples; very little art was made for private use.

By traditional aesthetic standards, the products of the Cultural Revolution were crude and amateurish—aesthetics were far less important than message. The unprecedented surge in propaganda from all quarters—centralized and ad hoc—can be compared to the combined effect of mainstream and guerrilla promotional campaigns, where impact, not necessarily quality, is the greatest virtue.

destroying the old

The Cultural Revolution called for a drastic transformation of China's cultural heritage. Red Guards swarmed through cities and countryside, denouncing the "Four Olds"—antiquated ideas, culture, customs, and habits. They viciously punished the "Stinking Ninth": Party members, educators, and intellectuals who questioned Maoist thought were accused of "cultural pollution." The Red Terror, as these rampages were called, shattered much of Chinese culture. Temples and schools were destroyed, paintings and books burned, monuments razed.

One technique favored by the Red Guards was public humiliation. Discredited party leaders were paraded through the streets or forced to stand or kneel, head bowed, in public places for excruciatingly long periods, with dunce caps on their heads and demeaning signs around their necks scrawled with insults such as "counterrevolutionary intellectual," "traitor and thief," or "spy." The Red Guards were given extralegal powers to act both violently and irrationally. Street names in the city were changed, thus throwing traffic in Beijing into chaos. (At least one Red Guard cadre took the Communist anthem, "The East Is Red," so literally that he demanded that traffic in Beijing proceed on red and stop on green.)

迎接全国科学大会的召开

383. *Aviation Knowledge*
The military became
a key part of Chinese
culture. Periodicals
like this aviation
magazine propagated
the Communist ideal of
service to the state.
1978

384. Notebook
Propaganda images
were also common
on school textbooks
and notebooks.
c. 1969

385. *High Work*
This workers' magazine
cover features Mao in
a quasi-religious pose
floating in a sea of
red flags.
c. 1966

386. *Dragon Lake Wave*
Literature was as
politicized as ballet and
opera. This became a
popular novel during
the Cultural Revolution.
1965

387. Red Guard armband
The Red Guards wore
green uniforms adorned
only with a Mao badge
and red armband,
inscribed with the
characters *hong* (red)
wei (protect) *bing*
(soldier), or "red guards."
The official stamp identi-
fies this armband as
belonging to a member
of the Shanghai Worker
Rebellion Group.
1967

Background:
Men and women
accused of being
counterrevolutionaries
are paraded through
the streets of Beijing
wearing dunce caps with
demeaning inscriptions.
1967

Before the Cultural Revolution, the Central Committee controlled everything, including propaganda. After 1966, Mao created four elite groups that reported directly to him. Three of them were organized special interest groups representing the Party, the government, and the army. The fourth, the Cultural Revolution Small Group, was semiofficial at first but developed into a formal group. It took charge of cultural matters. "Mao Zedong Thought" was emblazoned on posters, badges, pins, signs, banners, textiles, and porcelains. Most of the propaganda was produced by the Revolutionary Rebel Corps, an offshoot of the Red Guards. The provincial revolutionary organizing committees had considerable autonomy in producing posters, banners, books, and sculptures. At the same time, Red Guard artists spontaneously took their own artwork directly to printers, which produced materials at cost, as an act of patriotism. Red Guard cadres were invested with the task of distributing posters or leaflets.

Outside China's borders, Mao was romanticized by the radical left in Europe and the United States for his revolutionary stance, viewed as the champion of a Third World revolution that would free workers and peasants from the shackles of colonialist European nations. Though little information was published about the reality of the Cultural Revolution, some Western supporters of the People's Republic began expressing indignation at China's increasingly ruthless cultural policies. The renowned leftist British art critic Herbert Read wrote in 1968 in the otherwise sympathetic *China Policy Study Group* newsletter, "The artistic consequences are disastrous from any conceivable standard of aesthetic judgment.... [Illustrations] are now all as dreary as commercial posters in a capitalist country....It becomes clear what a cultural revolution would mean in [England]— the closing and perhaps the destruction of the National Gallery and the Tate Gallery and the elevation of Madame Tussaud's to national status."[9] In response, an anonymous Chinese cultural official wrote in the *China Daily*, "In Western society today, artistic form often takes precedence over content, lack of which is regarded by many as a virtue....In China, content takes precedence over form, but [this] does not mean that the latter is brushed aside....If revolutionary artists in China today can succeed in producing truly universal art, so much the better."[10]

As Mao feared, the quest for universal art failed to produce lasting genius, but it did serve its political purpose: to provoke millions of Chinese into attacking each other in a defamatory chaos, above which Mao alone towered.

386

387

上海工人革命造反总司令部
造反队
编号 521092

黎白著
龙潭波涛
中国少年儿童出版社

388

无产阶级文化大革命全面胜利万岁

selling the cultural revolution

big-character posters

Not all Chinese traditional arts and crafts were expunged. Mao, like Hitler and Mussolini, claimed the artist's mantle. He was a poet and a master calligrapher who took pride in his expert hand. His brushed characters were copied onto armbands worn by the Red Guards, and an example of his calligraphy hangs in his mausoleum in Beijing. Mao actively encouraged calligraphy, which was a long-revered art in China.

At the 1965 Yan'an Forum on Literature and Art, Mao proclaimed that while the new China was an anti-imperialist, antifeudal culture governed by the proletariat, not all of the "old ways"—calligraphy among them—were counterrevolutionary.[11] The Chinese should not "refuse to utilize the literary and artistic forms of the past," he said, "but in our hands these old forms, remolded and infused with new content ... become something revolutionary in the service of the people."[12] He cautioned, however, that "uncritical transplantation or copying from the ancients and the foreigners is the most sterile and harmful dogmatism in literature and art."[13] The same year, the Chinese poet Lu Xun made the point that "in adopting old forms, something must be excised ... other things must be added in. The result is the appearance of a new form, and that is change."[14]

The most widespread graphic tool at the outset of the Cultural Revolution was the *dazibao*, as the Communist Chinese called it—a calligraphed, newspaper-like wall hanging known in English as a "big-character poster." It had no official format, though the words on it were usually black or red Chinese characters handwritten on white or red backgrounds. The posters, hung in factories and public buildings or posted on the streets, provided up-to-the-minute "news"; they included praise of Mao, admonitions against counterrevolutionary activities, as well as revolutionary slogans such as "Let a hundred flowers bloom, let a hundred schools of thought contend"; "To rebel is justified"; "Seek truth from facts"; and "Dare to think, dare to act." Mao's famous "Bombard the headquarters" *dazibao*, written in his own recognizable hand, was emblazoned with the inflammatory slogan "To rebel is justified" and hung at Peking University.

The first *dazibao* was published in 1957, during the Hundred Flowers campaign,[15] the somewhat cynically titled period during which Mao encouraged criticism of the Communist party—largely as a means to identify party critics prior to purging them. That same year, hundreds of thousands of placards were hung at Peking University. A contemporary witness exclaimed, "At no time, in the entire course of Chinese history—indeed in the history of any nation in the world—has such a medium of communication been so widely used and shrewdly manipulated."[16] During the Great Leap Forward, *dazibao* were the principle means of mass communication and indoctrination. In 1963

Mao wrote, "*Dazibao* is, under the present conditions, the best form of [propaganda] which is beneficial for the proletariat but damaging to the bourgeois…. The more we use, the better."[17] During the Cultural Revolution, the number of *dazibao* increased exponentially.

Dazibao were large, one-off, handwritten posters. They were complemented by *xiaozibao* ("small-character posters"), which were smaller and usually set in type, and *meishu dazibao* ("illustrated posters"), usually also produced as one-offs. Printed posters were produced in large quantities by the Central Command Printing Company, the Shanghai People's Art Publishing House, and the Jiangxi Art Publishing House, among others. They were generally printed on cheap, flimsy paper; metal type was used for the characters; and matte inks often soaked through the paper, resulting in a slightly washed-out look. Some were two-color woodcuts, others were quite detailed and technically proficient. In contrast to the *dazibao*, these were mass-produced and sold cheaply

in stores like the New China Bookstore, a national chain. In addition to their propagandist purposes, they were used to decorate rooms, replacing the more traditional Chinese symbols for longevity, happiness, and prosperity.

Although posters made in the later period of the Cultural Revolution tended to be more festive and less polemical, Socialist Realism remained the dominant genre. Sometimes color photographs of Mao and his fellow party members were used, but they were invariably heavily airbrushed. In any color reproduction, only certain hues of red, yellow, and orange were acceptable.

jiang qing and the performing arts

The performing arts—in particular the reformed Beijing Opera—played an important role in setting the tone for the revolutionary style. In 1966 Mao created the Central Committee's Cultural Revolution Group, which included Chen Boda, editor in chief

IMMORTAL HERO YANG KEN-SZE

A position covered by seven hidden pillboxes was occupied by Ken-sze and his comrades. The Kuomintang captives couldn't believe that such a small force of PLA men could seize a position defended by an entire reinforced company.

The great Huai-Hai Campaign ended in victory. On April 21, 1949, a million PLA men crossed the Yangtse River to liberate their suffering countrymen in the south.

of the Communist newspapers *Red Flag* and *People's Daily*; Lin Biao, minister of defense; and Mao's wife, Jiang Qing, the former movie actress who became de facto minister of public enlightenment. Madame Mao steered many aspects of the propaganda effort from her ministry in Beijing. With her associates Wang Hongwen, Yao Wenyuan, and Zhang Chunqiao—the "Gang of Four"—she controlled all cultural activities, especially film as well as her famed Beijing operas and ballets. These pedantic political messages set to music and dance, included repeated performances of the so-called Eight Model Operas, such as *The Legend of the Red Lantern* and the ballet

of the *Red Women's Detachment*. Jiang Qing and her acolytes were largely responsible for propelling the Cultural Revolution into a vicious cycle of violence and arbitrary purges. Immediately after Mao's death in 1976, the Gang of Four was attacked by the population. They were later tried and condemned to death (Jiang Qing's execution was later commuted to a life sentence, and she died in 1991).

picture-story books

One of the prodigious media of the early years of the Cultural Revolution was the comic book (or, as it

393–95. *Immortal Hero Yang Ken-sze*
"Picture-story" books were a common means of disseminating information in China and abroad. *Immortal Hero Yang Ken-sze,* written by Wang Hao and Yi Fan with drawings by He Youzhi recounts the story of a Chinese soldier who fought against the United States during the Korean War. It was translated into English and published by the Foreign Languages Press. 1965

was known, "picture-story book"), an enormous number of which were produced in small-format paperback. These were used to reach children and the illiterate masses, and usually depicted heroic Communist tales of Mao's Long March and resistance against the Japanese. The style was linear, gestural, and representational, not unlike conventional Western children's books. In 1958, the first year of the Great Leap Forward, more than 1,600 comics were published, mostly about revolutionary struggle and socialist construction. "Picture-story books are not only favorites with children and adults who can only read a little," wrote journalist Jiang Weipu in

Chinese Literature in 1959, "but even well-educated readers skim through the best of them when they have leisure."[18] The stories of heroism and devotion were rendered simply and printed on inexpensive paper. The Cultural Revolution did not mark a significant shift in picture-book design; the publications continued to be cheaply produced and distributed in China and abroad in multiple languages.

porcelain figurines
Of all the Communist Chinese propagandist memorabilia, the most curious are the thousands

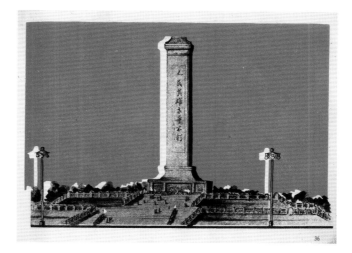

396–405. Propaganda art primer
This textbook teaches young students how to create visual propaganda—calligraphy, posters, signs, and symbols—in the service of the Cultural Revolution. These images are realized in brush and ink and woodcut. 1967

of colorful porcelain figurines that depict political leaders and popular heroes, often in revolutionary action. These statuettes—produced by "rehabilitated" artisans in workshops throughout China—were usually given as souvenirs to loyal revolutionary functionaries. Recipients so honored were expected to give them prominent display.

Among the large variety of figures depicted were peasants, workers, Red Guards, ballet dancers, and soldiers in all manner of social and political interaction—with Little Red Books, flags, banners, signs, and guns. Many figurines were based on characters in Madame Mao's operas and affect the

heroic stances that became characteristic of the Chinese ballet during this era. One figurine in particular shows two workers astride a (distinctly phallic) silver missile, holding a scroll inscribed with the words "Surpass U.S. and U.K."—summing up Mao's military plans.

The hand-painted statuettes, baked with a shiny glaze, stand in stark contrast to the brutal reality they portray. The most disconcerting feature Red Guards, factory workers, and peasants perpetrating cruel—though officially sanctioned—acts of humiliation on petit bourgeoisie, landowners, and other "social criminals," shown on their

406–412. Revolutionary
ceramics
Porcelain figurines,
produced between 1966
and 1975, were created
by various Red Guard
groups as commemorative
souvenirs: Workers
astride a Chinese rocket
hold a sign that reads
"Surpass U.S. and U.K.,"
a slogan coined during
the Great Leap Forward
(406); Red Guards
punish an intellectual
wearing a dunce cap
that says "Stinking Ninth
Category" (407); Mao
saluting, wearing his
People's Liberation Army
(PLA) coat (408); female
soldier in the home guard
militia (409); young Red
Guard holding Mao's
Little Red Book (410);
Mao surrounded by Red
Guards and children in
this commemoration of
his famous swim in the
Yangtze River on 16 July
1966, which marked
his political resurgence
(411); members of the
proletariat—a peasant
woman, a factory worker,
a PLA soldier—with a
young Red Guard (412).

knees, wearing dunce caps, with signs hanging from their necks.

Some artists were employed by government-sponsored Ceramic and Porcelain Research Centers, but many collaborated directly with Red Guard cadres to create new designs for statues and figurines that would compete with those produced by the official provincial workshops. There was no limit to the figures depicted: from statues of Communist leaders to what were known as "model citizens," heroes of the revolution, such as Wang Jinxi, the "model factory worker," and Chen Yonggui, "the model farmer," as well as depictions of children in school uniforms worshipping at the feet of Mao. Some ceramics were based on larger sculptural templates, such as an enormous monument in northern China titled *The Rent Collector*—a sculptural frieze of many figures, which depicts the brutality of wealthy landowners to their peasants.

Ceramics is an age-old craft in China, and even though the Communists did their utmost to outlaw remnants of the imperial past, the familiar porcelain

medium was an effective way to promulgate Maoist messages. Porcelain was also a more practical material than metal, which was scarce in China at the time (Mao criticized artists for using metal in their work). Figurines could be manufactured inexpensively, and even in private kilns, in order not to waste manpower in overworked factories. In the all-out propaganda campaign—at a time when access to television and radio was limited—these quaint though politically charged souvenirs brought revolution from the street into the home.

propaganda abroad

The Communist Chinese also aimed their propaganda at Europe and North America. Periodicals such as *China Pictorial*—like *USSR in Construction*, printed in multiple languages—were illustrated with typical Chinese Socialist Realism on the covers and interiors, as well as heroic (often posed) photographs. The Foreign Languages Press in Beijing exported many of the printed items—posters, silk wall hangings,

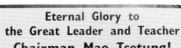
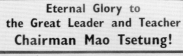

413

中國工人畫刊 3

Иллюстрированный журнал "КИТАЙСКИЕ РАБОЧИЕ"

中华全国总工会

1950.

CHINESE WORKERS' PICTORIAL

414

CHINA
PICTORIAL 1967 11

415

Eternal Glory to
the Great Leader and Teacher
Chairman Mao Tsetung!

China
Reconstructs

Double Issue
VOL. XXV NO. 11
NOVEMBER 1976
VOL. XXV NO. 12
DECEMBER 1976

416

NEW WOMEN in NEW CHINA

417

THE STORY OF
THE MODERN
PEKING OPERA
SHACHIAPANG

413–17. Foreign propaganda
The Foreign Languages Press was active in disseminating the words and pictures of Mao to sympathizers of the revolution around the world: This 1950 issue from *Chinese Workers' Pictorial* was aimed at readers in the Soviet Union (413); this 1967 issue of *China Pictorial* attempted to put a positive spin on the Cultural Revolution (414); *China Reconstructs* was one of the many periodicals promoting China's (failed) economic plans (415); *New Women in New China* promoted the role of women in Communist society (416); this is an English-language version of the popular opera *Shachiapang*, one of Jiang Qing's Eight Model Operas (417).

418. Mao postcards
Mao's image was sold in many forms, including this portfolio of photos for export.
1967

419. *Red Women's Detachment*
Another popular example of the Eight Model Operas.
1966

Background:
Westerners demonstrate in favor of Mao's Cultural Revolution.
1976

picture storybooks, and periodicals—through their retail outlets, including China Books and Periodicals and the U.S.–China People's Friendship Association. Even the largest posters and wall hangings never cost more than one dollar in the United States.

By the mid-1970s, after almost a decade of cultural upheaval, Mao's enemies in the Communist party had been eliminated, orchestrated chaos had taken its toll, and Red Guard members were growing older. As the Cultural Revolution began winding down, Communist propaganda replaced internal enemies with outside imperialist and capitalist threats, and calls to liberate Taiwan. China turned much of its foreign policy toward the Third World, where it used propaganda (as well as its weapons) to foment revolution.

UPHOLD CHAIRMAN MAO'S

REVOLUTIONARY LINE!

UPHOLD CHAIRMAN MAO'S

REVOLUTIONARY

我们的伟大领袖毛主席

OUR GREAT LEADER
CHAIRMAN MAO

NOTRE GRAND DIRIGEANT,
LE PRESIDENT MAO

NUESTRO GRAN LIDER
EL PRESIDENTE MAO

RED WOMEN'S DETACHMENT

end of the brand

In July 1974, China's economic decline and deepening chaos caused Mao to shift his loyalties toward Zhou Enlai and Deng Xiaoping (who had earlier been denounced, but was now "rehabilitated"). Deng assumed increasing power, starting in the summer of 1974.[19] The aging Mao voluntarily withdrew from the propaganda spotlight, and proxies emerged in his place. Comrade Lei Feng, a presumably real but idealized People's Liberation Army soldier, became the poster boy for the self-sacrificing spirit of China. An orphan, Lei was said to have been raised by the Communist party; he died very young, reportedly in the line of duty. Lei's story was built around his ordinariness. He became a martyr for doing nothing but faithfully serving the People's Republic. Lei's myth was created through numerous diaries allegedly written by him, chronicling his and his comrades' service. As Mao's image became less prominent, he was replaced by Lei Feng.

The Cultural Revolution had tragic consequences for China. The political instability brought about by shifts in economic policy resulted in diminished national growth, and years of social upheaval left the country in chaos. Millions of party members and wrongfully purged citizens had lost their foothold in society. Many who experienced the Cultural Revolution while in their teens and early twenties did not receive an education, and as China moved into the future, they were left behind. The reality of the Cultural Revolution stands in stark contrast to the fantasy the propagandists presented so efficiently. In the end the reams of paper, the tons of badges, and the warehouses of figurines amounted to little more than historical kitsch.

Shortly after Mao's death on 9 September 1976, Deng became the leader of China and declared at the Chinese Communist Party's Eleventh Party Congress that the Cultural Revolution had come to an end. He sought to address the responsibility of the party in this tragedy. He portrayed Mao as a misguided hero who, nonetheless, was a great proletarian revolutionary. The party's triumphs continued to rest heavily on Mao's achievements. Unlike the Soviets, the Chinese had no Lenin as the "father of the revolution" to underpin the legitimacy of their regime. Mao was Lenin and Stalin in one. Had he been discredited at that point in history, the entire state would have fallen under a cloud. Deng's resolution absolved Mao from the worst crimes of the Cultural Revolution, while laying the blame on Lin Biao, Jiang Qing, and other "opportunists." The Cultural Revolution was devastating, yet the cult of Mao continued, and still exists in a more benevolent form. Today Mao's image is viewed as benignly as Lenin's, a testament to how branding can trump reality.

Opposite:
A propaganda poster after the fall of the Gang of Four—the high officials blamed for the worst excesses of the Cultural Revolution after the death of Mao—depicts the "gang" impaled and burning, their human heads on the bodies of animals. They are (left to right) Yao Wenyuan, Wang Hongwen, Zhang Chunqiao, and Jiang Qing, Mao's widow.

notes

introduction

1. Aldous Huxley, *Brave New World Revisited* (1958; repr., New York: Harper & Row, 1965), 43.
2. Ibid., 47.
3. Ibid., 45.
4. Ibid., 53.
5. Ibid., 15.

chapter 1: the nazis

1. Eugen Hadamovsky, *Propaganda and National Power* (New York: Arno Press, 1972), 19.
2. Erwin Schockel, *Das politische Plakat* (Munich: Zentralverlag der NSDAP/Franz Eher Verlag, 1939).
3. Adolf Hitler, *Mein Kampf* (New York: Houghton Mifflin, 1999), 492.
4. Ibid.
5. Ibid., 495.
6. Frederic Spotts, *Hitler and the Power of Aesthetics* (New York: Overlook Press, 2003), 50.
7. Hitler, *Mein Kampf*, 495.
8. Ibid., 496.
9. Ibid.
10. Ibid.
11. Ibid., 497.
12. Steven Heller, *The Swastika: Symbol Beyond Redemption?* (New York: Allworth Press, 2000), 40.
13. *Swastika* was published by Curtis Publishing in Philadelphia between 1914 and 1918.
14. Nicholas Goodrick-Clarke, *The Occult Roots of Nazism: Secret Aryan Cults and Their Influence on Nazi Ideology* (New York: New York University Press, 1992), 90–99.
15. Ibid., 165.
16. Associated Press, October 1944.
17. Deffke's assistant to Paul Rand, 1980, Paul Rand Archive, Yale University.
18. Hitler, *Mein Kampf*, 495.
19. Fritz Morstein Marx, "State Propaganda in Germany," in Harwood Lawrence Childs, ed., *Propaganda and Dictatorship: A Collection of Papers* (New York: Arno Press, 1972), 17.
20. Z.A.B. Zeman, *Nazi Propaganda* (London: Oxford University Press, 1964), 10.
21. *New York Times,* 14 March 1934.
22. Ibid., January 1934.
23. Roderick Stackelberg and Sally Anne Winkle, *The Nazi Sourcebook: An Anthology of Texts* (London and New York: Routlege, 2002), 186–87.
24. Marx, "State Propaganda," 18.
25. Hadamovsky, *Propaganda,* 182.
26. Marx, "State Propaganda," 18.
27. Ibid., 19.
28. Ibid., 18.
29. Zeman, *Nazi Propaganda*, 3.
30. Hoffman introduced Hitler to Eva Braun, who became his mistress. Angela Lambert, *The Lost Life of Eva Braun* (New York: St. Martin's Press, 2007).
31. Marx, "State Propaganda," 16.
32. Fritz Morstein Marx, *Government in the Third Reich* (New York: McGraw-Hill, 1936), 100.
33. Adolf Hitler, Interview with the Associated Press, 1934.
34. Hadamovsky, *Propaganda,* 10.
35. Hildegard Brenner, "Art in the Political Power Struggle, 1933–34," in Hajo Holborn, ed., *Republic to Reich: The Making of the Nazi Revolution* (New York: Pantheon Books, 1972), 411.
36. "Writing and Lettering in the Service of the New State," *Die zeitgemäße Schrift* 36 (January 1936), 39.
37. Brenner, "Political Power Struggle," 423.
38. Ibid., 69.
39. One of the specimen cards included in the portfolio within the book listed the face as "Futura" and credited it to Renner, who had been relieved of his teaching post at the Munich Meisterschule for being politically undesirable.
40. Brenner, "Political Power Struggle," 424.
41. Hellmut Lehmann-Haupt, *Art Under a Dictatorship* (New York: Oxford University Press, 1954), 172.

42. Hadamovsky, *Propaganda,* 4.

43. Ibid., 8.

44. Ibid., 6–7.

45. The Nazis were not the first to use this shorthand: the Soviets introduced rhythmic contractions like *agitprop* (agitation and propaganda) and turned the mouthful Komitet Gosudarstvennoy Bezopasnosti (Committee for State Security) into KGB, which was a descendant of Cheka (the abbreviation for *vecheka*, itself an acronym for All-Russian Extraordinary Committee to Combat Counterrevolution and Sabotage).

46. Andreas Fleischer and Frank Kämpfer, "The Political Poster in the Third Reich," in *The Nazification of Art: Art, Design, Music, Architecture and Film in the Third Reich,* ed. Brandon Taylor and Wilfried van der Will (Winchester, England: The Winchester Press, 1990), 184.

47. This poster bears a startling resemblance to the 1963 cover photograph by Robert Freeman, who was influenced by photographs by Astrid Kirchherr, for the album *Meet the Beatles* (in the U.K., *With the Beatles*), though it is doubtful that either photographer was directly influenced by Hoffmann's photograph.

48. Fleischer and Kämpfer, "Political Poster," 190.

49. Robert Edwin Herzstein, *The War that Hitler Won: The Most Infamous Propaganda Campaign in History* (New York: Putnam, 1978), 198.

50. *Gebrauchsgraphik* 10, no. 1 (1933): 18.

51. Zeman, *Nazi Propaganda*, 23.

52. Primo Levi, *The Drowned and the Saved* (New York: Vintage International, 1989), 119.

chapter 2: the italian fascists

1. Simonetta Falasca-Zamponi, *Fascist Spectacle: The Aesthetics of Power in Mussolini's Italy* (Berkeley and Los Angeles: University of California Press, 1997), 39.

2. Herman Finer, *Mussolini's Italy: A Classic Study of the Non-Communist One-Party State* (1935; repr., New York: Universal Library/Grosset & Dunlapp, 1965), 148.

3. Falasca-Zamponi, *Fascist Spectacle*, 117. Ciano was executed for treason on 11 January 1944.

4. William Ebenstein, *Fascist Italy* (New York: American Book Company, 1939), 280.

5. Herbert L. Matthews, *The Fruits of Fascism* (New York: Harcourt, Brace, 1943), 187.

6. Finer, *Mussolini's Italy*, 103.

7. Matthews, *Fruits of Fascism,* 71.

8. Edward R. Tannenbaum, *The Fascist Experience: Italian Society and Culture, 1922–1945* (New York: Basic Books, 1972), 70.

9. Matthews, *Fruits of Fascism,* 201.

10. Falasca-Zamponi, *Fascist Spectacle,* 92.

11. Ibid., 97.

12. David Cundy, "Marinetti and Italian Futurist Typography," *Art Journal* 41, no. 4 (Winter 1981): 349–52.

13. Steven Heller and Georgette Ballance, *Graphic Design History* (New York: Allworth Press, 2001), 154.

14. Ibid., 155.

15. Matthews, *Fruits of Fascism,* 101.

chapter 3: the soviet communists

1. John Reed, *Ten Days that Shook the World* (Mineola, N.Y.: Dover, 2006).

2. Terence M. O'Keefe, "Ideology and the Protestant Principle," *Journal of the American Academy of Religion* 51, no. 2 (June 1983): 283–305.

3. "The origin of the Soviet's red flag…has been variously attributed to a 16th century peasant rally, to a revolt nearly a hundred years later, to a farmer's uprising in 1876." In prerevolutionary Russia, red was a sign that a town or village was besieged by disease. A. Guy Hope and Janet Barker Hope, *Symbols of the Nations* (Washington, D.C.: Public Affairs Press, 1973), 274.

4. *The Flag Bulletin* XI, no. 1 (Winchester, Mass.: The Flag Research Center, 1972), 43–53.

5. V. I. Lenin, *Collected Works* (Moscow: Progress Publishers, 1965), 44–49. See also C. Vaughan James, *Soviet Socialist Realism: Origins and Theory* (New York: St. Martin's Press, 1973), app. 1, 103.

6. Matthew Cullerne Bown, *Art under Stalin* (New York: Holmes & Meier Publishers, 1991), 24.

7. Ibid., 20.

8. Brandon Taylor, *Art and Literature under the*

Bolsheviks: The Crisis of Renewal (London: Pluto Press, 1991), 88.

9. Margot Lovejoy, *Digital Currents: Art in the Electronic Age* (London and New York: Routledge, 2004), 38.

10. The New Typography was the brainchild of German graphic and type designer Jan Tschichold. In 1925 Tschichold edited a special issue of a printing trade journal called *Typographische Mitteilungen: Zeitschrift des Bildungsverbandes der Deutschen Buchdrucker* dedicated to what he termed *Elementare Typographie*, which included the new asymmetrical method of composing type, largely influenced by Constructivism and later taught at the Bauhaus. In 1928 he authored the book *Die Neue Typographie*, which set out the primary rules for how to design and compose using this new method, which by then had taken hold in Holland, Eastern Europe, Germany, and even Italy.

11. Michael Patrick Hearn, unpublished manuscript.

12. Ibid.

13. In his as yet unpublished manuscript on the epoch, Hearn dubs this period the golden age of children's book publishing in Russia.

14. Evgeny Steiner, *Stories for Little Comrades: Revolutionary Artists and the Making of Early Soviet Children's Books* (Seattle: University of Washington Press, 1999), 174–75.

15. Bown, *Art under Stalin*, 29.

16. Ibid., 175.

17. This is vividly exhibited in the collection of photographs by scholar of Soviet graphics David King in *The Commissar Vanishes* (New York: Metropolitan Books, 1997).

18. Charles Harrison and Paul Woods, eds., *Art in Theory, 1900–2000: An Anthology of Changing Ideas* (New York: Wiley/Blackwell, 2002), 403.

19. Henri Arvon, *Marxist Esthetics* (Ithaca, N.Y.: Cornell University Press, 1973), 86.

20. Ibid., 85.

21. Bernard Smith, *Modernism's History: A Study in Twentieth-century Art and Ideas* (New Haven, Conn.: Yale University Press, 1998), 206.

chapter 4: the communist chinese

1. Seymour Topping, *Journey Between Two Chinas* (New York: Harper and Row, 1974), 201.

2. Lu Na, *The Badges of Chairman Mao* (Beijing: Guoji Wenhua Chuban She, 1993), 4–5.

3. Li Zhisui, *The Private Life of Chairman Mao: The Memoirs of Mao's Personal Physician* (New York: Random House, 1994), 517.

4. A. Guy Hope and Janet Barker Hope, *Symbols of the Nations* (Washington, D.C.: Public Affairs Press, 1973), 279.

5. Ralph C. Crozier, *China's Cultural Legacy and Communism* (New York: Praeger Publishers, 1970), 15.

6. Zhong Zhao, *The Communist Program for Literature and Art in China* (1955; repr., Hong Kong: Union Research Institute, 1962), 27.

7. Ibid., 29.

8. Ibid., 30.

9. Crozier, *China's Cultural Legacy*, 296–97.

10. Ibid., 269.

11. Ibid., 15–16.

12. Ibid., 15.

13. Ibid., 16.

14. Ibid., 18.

15. The term comes from a speech delivered by then propaganda chief Lu Tingyi, "Let a hundred flowers bloom, let a hundred schools of thought contend." In Frederick T.C. Yu, *Mass Persuasion in Communist China* (New York: Frederick A. Praeger, 1964), 137.

16. Yu, *Mass Persuasion in Communist China*, 138.

17. Ibid., 137.

18. Crozier, *China's Cultural Legacy,* 164.

19. In the fall of 1975, hard-liners convinced Mao that Deng's policies would eventually lead to the repudiation of the Cultural Revolution. Mao shifted again, and authorized criticism of Deng by means of *dazibao*. Deng was formally purged in April, but Mao's death in September 1976 saved him from execution, and he reemerged as leader in 1977.

Adam, Peter. *Art of the Third Reich*. New York: Harry N. Abrams, 1992.

Aly, Gotz. *Hitler's Beneficiaries: Plunder, Racial War, and the Nazi Welfare State*. New York: Metropolitan Books, 2007.

Anti-Defamation League. *The Skinhead International: A Worldwide Survey of Neo-Nazi Skinheads*. New York: Anti-Defamation League, 1995.

Arendt, Hannah. *The Origins of Totalitarianism*. New York: Shocken Books, 2004.

Arvon, Henri. *Marxists Esthetics*. Ithaca, NY: Cornell University Press, 1973.

Atkins, Jacqueline M., ed. *Wearing Propaganda: Textiles on the Home Front in Japan, Britain, and the United States, 1931–1945*. New Haven, CT: Yale University Press, 2005.

Aulich, James, and Marta Sylvestrovà. *Political Posters in Central and Eastern Europe 1945–95*. Manchester, England: Manchester University Press, 2000.

Bachrach, Susan D. *The Nazi Olympics: Berlin, 1936*. Boston: Little, Brown, and Co., 2000.

Bartoletti, Susan Campbell. *Hitler Youth: Growing up in Hitler's Shadow*. New York: Scholastic, 2005.

Becker, Lutz, and Richard Hollis. *Avant-Garde Graphics 1918–1934: From the Merrill C. Berman Collection*. London: Hayward Gallery, 1984.

Bendavid-Val, Leah. *Propaganda & Dreams: Photographing the 1930s in the USSR and the US*. Zurich and New York: Edition Stemmle, 1999.

Ben-Ghiat, Ruth. *Fascist Modernities: Italy, 1922–1945*. Berkeley and Los Angeles: University of California Press, 2001.

Bernays, Edward. *Propaganda*. New York: Ig Publishing, 1928.

Bloch, Marc. *Strange Defeat: A Statement of Evidence Written in 1940*. London: W. W. Norton, 1968.

Bosworth, R.J.B. *Mussolini's Italy: Life Under the Dictatorship, 1915–1945*. New York: Penguin Books, 2005.

Bown, Matthew Cullerne. *Art Under Stalin*. New York: Holmes & Meier Publishers, 1991.

Brilli, Attilio. *Immagini E Retorica Di Regime: Bozzetti Originali Di Propaganda Fascista, 1935–1942*. Milan: Federico Motta Editore, 2001.

Bytwerk, Randall L. *Bending Spines: The Propagandas of Nazi Germany and the German Democratic Republic*. East Lansing, MI: Michigan State University Press, 2004.

Cesarani, David. *Becoming Eichmann*. Cambridge, MA: Da Capo Press, 2004.

Chang, Jung, and Jon Halliday. *Mao: The Unknown Story*. New York: Alfred A. Knopf, 2005.

Childs, Harwood Lawrence, ed. *Propaganda and Dictatorship: A Collection of Papers*. New York: Arno Press, 1972.

Chinese Propaganda Posters from the Collection of Michael Wolf. Cologne, Germany: Taschen, 2003.

Clark, Tody. *Art and Propaganda in the Twentieth Century*. New York: Harry N. Abrams, 1997.

Clough, Rosa Trillo. *Futurism, The Story of a Modern Art Movement: A New Appraisal*. New York: Philosophical Library, 1961.

Corney, Frederick C. *Telling October: Memory and the Making of the Bolshevik Revolution*. Ithaca, N.Y.: Cornell University Press, 2004.

Cowdery, Ray, and Josephine Cowdery. *German Print Advertising, 1933–1945*. South Dakota: USM, 2004.

—. *Masters of Ceremony*. Minnesota: USM, 1998.

—. *Papers Please! Identity Documents, Permits and Authorizations of the Third Reich*. Minnesota: USM, 1996.

Crozier, Ralph C. *China's Cultural Legacy and Communism*. New York: Praeger Publishers, 1970.

Cruickshank, Charles. *The Fourth Arm: Psychological Warfare 1938–1945*. New York: Oxford University Press, 1981.

Cundy, David. "Marinetti and Italian Futurist Typography." In *Art Journal* 41, no. 4, 1981.

Cushing, Lincoln, and Ann Tompkins. *Chinese Posters:*

Art from the Great Proletarian Cultural Revolution. San Francisco: Chronicle Books, 2007.

Czech, Hans-Jörg, and Nikola Doll, eds. *Kunst und Propaganda: Im Streit der Nationen, 1930–1945,* Dresden, Germany: Sandstein, 2007.

Davis, Brian L. *Uniforms and Insigna of the Luftwaffe.* London: Arms and Armour, London, 1991.

De Grazia, Victoria. *The Culture of Consent: Mass Organization of Leisure in Fascist Italy.* New York: Cambridge University Press, 1981.

De Micheli, Mario. *Manifesti Rivoluzionari: Europa 1900–1940.* Milan: Fratelli Fabbri Editori, 1973.

Dornberg, John. *Munich 1973: The Story of Hitler's First Grab for Power.* New York: Harper & Row, 1982.

Ebenstein, William. *Fascist Italy.* New York: American Book Company, 1939.

Edison, Victoria, and James Edison. *Cultural Revolution Posters & Memorabilia.* Lancaster, PA: Schiffer Publishing, 2005.

Evans, Harriet, and Stephanie Donald, eds. *Picturing Power in the People's Republic of China: Posters of the Cultural Revolution.* Lanham, MD: Rowman & Littlefield, 1999.

Evans, Richard J. *The Third Reich in Power.* New York: Penguin Books, 2006.

Fabre, Giorgio. *Hitler's Contract: How Mussolini Became the Führer's Publisher. The History of the Italian Edition of Mein Kampf.* New York: Enigma Books, 2006.

—. *Mussolini razzista. Dal socialismo al fascismo: la formazione di un antisemita.* Milan: Garzanti, 2005.

Falasca-Zamponi, Simonetta. *Fascist Spectacle: The Aesthetics of Power in Mussolini's Italy.* Berkeley and Los Angeles: University of California Press, 2000.

Fest, Joachim. *Speer: The Final Verdict.* Florida: Harcourt, 2001.

Feuchtwanger, E.J. *From Weimar to Hitler: Germany, 1918–33.* New York: St. Martin's Press, 1995.

Finer, Herman. *Mussolini's Italy: A Classic Study of the Non-Communist, One-Party State.* New York: Grosset & Dunlap, 1965.

Flag Research Center. *The Flag Bulletin* XI. New York: International Arts & Sciences Press, 1972.

Flores, Marcello. *Storia illustrata del comunismo.* Florence, Italy: Giunti Editore, 2003.

Franzinelli, Mimmo, and Emanuele V. Marino. *Il Duce proibito. Le fotografie di Mussolini che gli italiani non hanno mai visto.* Milan: Mondadori, 2003.

Fraser, Stewart E. *100 Great Chinese Posters: Recent Examples of "The People's Art" From The People's Republic of China.* New York: Images Graphiques, 1977.

Friedländer, Saul. *Reflections of Nazism: An Essay on Kitsch and Death.* New York: Harper & Row, 1984.

—. *The Years of Extermination: Nazi Germany and the Jews, 1939–1945.* New York: Harper Collins, 2007.

Fülöp-Miller, René. *The Mind and Face of Bolshevism: An Examination of Cultural Life in Soviet Russia.* New York: Putnam, 1927.

Gallo, Max. *Mussolini's Italy: Twenty Years of the Fascist Era.* New York: Macmillan, 1973.

Garruba, Caió. *Russian Revolutionary Posters, 1917–1929.* New York: Grove Press, 1967.

Gay, Peter. *Weimar Culture: The Outsider as Insider.* New York: W. W. Norton, 2001.

Germany: The Olympic Year. Berlin: Volk und Reich Verlag, 1936.

Golomstock, Igor. *Totalitarian Art in the Soviet Union, the Third Reich, Fascist Italy and the People's Republic of China.* London: Collins Harvill, 1990.

Goodrick-Clarke, Nicholas. *Hitler's Priestess: Savitri Devi, the Hindu-Aryan Myth, and Neo-Nazism.* New York: New York University Press, 1998.

—. *The Occult Roots of Nazism: Secret Aryan Cults and their Influence on Nazi Ideology: The Ariosophists of Austria and Germany, 1890–1935.* New York: New York University Press, 1992.

Grey, Paul, and Rosemarie Little. *Germany 1918–1945.* Cambridge: Cambridge University Press, 1997.

Guenther, Irene. *Nazi Chic? Fashioning Women in the Third Reich.* Oxford and New York: Berg, 2004.

Hadamovsky, Eugen. *Propaganda and National Power.* New York: Arno Press, 1972.

Harrison, Charles, and Paul Woods, eds. *Art in Theory, 1900–2000: An Anthology of Changing Ideas.* New York: Wiley/Blackwell, 2002.

Heller, Steven. *The Swastika: Symbol Beyond Redemption?* New York: Allworth Press, 2000.

Heller, Steven, and Georgette Ballance. *Graphic Design History.* New York: Allworth Press, 2001.

Herf, Jeffrey. *The Jewish Enemy: Nazi Propaganda During World War II and the Holocaust.* Cambridge, MA: Harvard University Press, 2006.

Herzstein, Robert Edwin. *The War That Hitler Won: The Most Infamous Propaganda Campaign in History.* New York: Putnam, 1978.

Hewitt, Andrew. *Fascist Modernism: Aesthetics, Politics, and the Avant-garde.* Stanford, CA: Stanford University Press, 1993.

Hinz, Berthold. *Art in the Third Reich.* New York: Pantheon Books, 1979.

Hitler, Adolf. *Mein Kampf.* New York: Houghton Mifflin, 1999.

Höhne, Heinz. *The Order of the Death's Head The Story of Hitler's SS.* London: Penguin Books, 1969.

Holborn, Hajo, ed. *Republic to Reich The Making of Nazi Revolution.* New York: Pantheon Books, 1972.

Hope, A. Guy, and Janet Barker Hope. *Symbols of the Nations.* Washington, D.C.: Public Affairs Press, 1973.

Huxley, Aldous. *Brave New World Revisited.* New York: Harper & Row, 1965.

Ingram, Philip. *Russia and the USSR, 1905–1991.* New York: Cambridge University Press, 1991.

James, C. Vaughan. *Soviet Socialist Realism: Origins and Theory.* New York: St. Martin's Press, 1973.

Jaubert, Alain. *Making People Disappear: An Amazing Chronicle of Photographic Deception.* Paris: Bernard Barrault, 1986.

Jowett, Garth S., and Victoria O'Donnell. *Propaganda and Persuasion.* Newbury Park, CA: Sage Publications, 1999.

Jubert, Roxane. *Typography and Graphic Design: From Antiquity to the Present.* Paris: Flammarion, 2006.

Kamenetsky, Christa. *Children's Literature in Hitler's Germany: The Cultural Policy of National Socialism.* Athens, OH: Ohio University Press, 1984.

Kaplan, Wendy, ed. *Designing Modernity: the Arts of Reform and Persuasion 1885–1945.* New York: Thames and Hudson, 1995.

Kapr, Albert. *Fraktur: Form und Geschichte der gebrochenen Schriften.* Mainz, Germany: H. Schmidt, 1993.

Kater, Michael H. *Hitler Youth.* Cambridge, MA: Harvard University Press, 2004.

Kellerhoff, Sven Felix. *Berlin Under the Swastika.* Berlin: Edition Q, 2006.

King, David. *The Commissar Vanishes: The Falsification of Photographs and Art in Stalin's Russia.* New York: Metropolitan Books, 1997.

Kirkpatrick, Ivone. *Mussolini: A Study in Power.* New York: Hawthorne Books, 1964.

Kitchen, Martin. *Nazi Germany: A Critical Introduction.* Stroud, England: Tempus Publishing, 2004.

Koepnick, Lutz. *Walter Benjamin and the Aesthetics of Power.* Lincoln, NE: University of Nebraska Press, 1999.

Koon, Tracy H. *Believe, Obey, Fight: Political Socialization of Youth in Fascist Italy, 1922–1943.* Chapel Hill, NC: University of North Carolina Press, 1985.

Kuromiya, Hiroaki. *Stalin.* Harlow, England and New York: Pearson/Longman, 2005.

La Bella, Andrea. *Nazismo.* Florence, Italy: Giunti Editore, 2001.

Laqueur, Walter. "Nazism and the Nazis: On Difficulties of Discovering the Whole Truth." In *Encounter* XXII. Germany: April 1964.

Lafont, Maria. *Soviet Posters: The Sergo Grigoria Collection.* New York: Prestel, 2007.

Lazzaro, Claudia, and Roger J. Crum, eds. *Donatello Among the Blackshirts: History and Modernity in the Visual Culture of Fascist Italy.* Ithaca, NY: Cornell University Press, 2005.

Lehmann-Haupt, Hellmut. *Art Under a Dictatorship.* New York: Oxford University Press, 1954.

Lenin, V. I. *Collected Works.* Moscow: Progress Publishers, 1965.

Levi, Primo. *Survival in Auschwitz.* New York: Touchstone, 1996.

—. *The Drowned and the Saved.* New York: Vintage International, 1989.

London, Kurt. *The Seven Soviet Arts.* New Haven, CT: Yale University Press, 1938.

MacFarquhar, Roderick, and Michael Schoenhals. *Mao's Last Revolution.* Cambridge, MA: Harvard University Press, 2006.

Rhodes, Anthony. *Propaganda: The Art of Persuasion World War II.* New Jersey: The Wellfleet Press, 1987.

Marks, Steven G. *How Russia Shaped the Modern World: From Art to Anti-Semitism, Ballet to Bolshevism.* Princeton, NJ: Princeton University Press, 2003.

Maser, Werner. *Hitler's Letters and Notes.* New York: Harper & Row, 1970.

Matthews, Herbert L. *The Fruits of Fascism.* New York: Harcourt, Brace, 1943.

Medvedev, Roy, and Zhores Medvedev. *The Unknown Stalin: His Life, Death, and Legacy.* New York: Overlook Press, 2004.

Montefiore, Simon Sebag. *Stalin: The Court of the Red Tsar.* New York: Alfred A.Knopf, 2004.

Marx, Fritz Morstein. *Government in the Third Reich.* New York: McGraw-Hill, 1936.

Moseley, Ray. *Mussolini: The Last 600 Days of Il Duce,* Lanham, MD: Taylor Trade Publishing, 2004.

Mosse, George L. *Masses and Man: Nationalist and Fascist Perceptions of Reality.* New York: H. Fertig, 1980.

—. *The Image of Man: The Creation of Modern Masculinity.* New York: Oxford University Press, 1996.

München: Haupstadt der Bewegung. Munich: Müncher Stadtmuseum, 1993.

Norris, Stephen M. *A War of Images: Russian Popular Prints, Wartime Culture, and National Identity, 1812–1945.* DeKalb, IL: Northern Illinois University Press, 2006.

Obrazu, Moc, and Moci Obrazu. *Power of Images, Images of Power.* Warsaw: Galerie U Krizovniku, 2005.

O'Keefe, Terence M. "Ideology and the Protestant Principle." In *Journal of the American Academy of Religion* 51, no. 2. June 1983.

Overy, Richard. *The Dictators: Hitler's Germany, Stalin's Russia.* New York: W. W. Norton, 2004.

Palla, Marco. *Fascismo.* Florence, Italy: Giunti Editore, 1997.

Palmér, Torsten, and Hendrik Neubauer. *The Weimar Republic Through the Lens of the Press.* Cologne, Germany: Könemann, 2000.

Pan, Lynn. *Mao Memorabilia: The Man and the Myth.* Hong Kong: Formasia Books, 1999.

Paxton, Robert O. *The Anatomy of Fascism.* New York: Vintage Books, 2005.

Payne, Stanley G. *A History of Fascism 1914–1945.* Madison, WI: The University of Wisconsin Press, 1995.

Pederson, Christian Fogd. *The International Flag Book in Color.* New York: William Morrow & Company, 1972.

Petropoulos, Jonathan. *Art as Politics in the Third Reich.* Chapel Hill, NC: The University of North Carolina Press, 1996.

—. *The Faustian Bargain: The Art World in Nazi Germany.* New York: Oxford University Press, 2000.

Phillips, Sir Percival. *The "Red" Dragon and the Black Shirts: How Italy Found Her Soul; The True Story of the Fascisti Movements.* London: Amalgamated Press, 1922.

Quinn, Malcolm. *The Swastika: Constructing the Symbol.* London, New York: Routledge, 1994.

Rabinach, Anson G. "The Aesthetics of Production in the Third Reich." In *Journal of Contemporary History* 11, No. 4. Newbury Park, CA: Sage Publications, 1976.

Reed, John. *Ten Days That Shook the World.* Mineola, NY: Dover, 2006.

Riboud, Marc. *The Three Banners of China.* New York: The Macmillan Company, 1966.

Rigg, Bryan Mark. *Hitler's Jewish Soldiers: The Untold Story of Nazi Racial Laws and Men of Jewish Descent in the German Military.* Lawrence, KS: University Press of Kansas, 2002.

Russo, Antonella. *Il fascismo in mostra.* Rome: Editori Riunitti, 1999.

Rutherford, Ward. *Hitler's Propaganda Machine.* London: Bison Books, 1978.

Schnapp, Jeffrey T., ed. *A Primer of Italian Fascism.* Lincoln, NE: University of Nebraska Press, 2000.

—. *Staging Fascism: 18 BL and the Theater of Masses for Masses.* Stanford, CA: Stanford University Press, 1996.

Segàla, Ariberto. *I muri Del Duce.* Gardolo, Italy: Edizioni Arca, 2001.

Short, Philip. *Mao: A Life.* China: China Youth Press, 1999.

Sigmann, Jean. *1848: The Romantic and Democratic Revolutions in Europe.* New York: Harper and Row, 1973.

Smith, Bernard. *Modernism's History: A Study in Twentieth-century Art and Ideas.* New Haven, CT: Yale University Press, 1998.

Spotts, Frederic. *Hitler and the Power of Aesthetics.* New York: Overlook Press, 2003.

Stackelberg, Roderick, and Sally Anne Winkle. *The Nazi Sourcebook: An Anthology of Texts.* London and New York: Routlege, 2002.

Steiner, Evgeny. *Stories for Little Comrades: Revolutionary Artists and the Making of Early Soviet Children's Books.* Seattle: University of Washington Press, 1999.

Steinweis, Alan E. *Art, Ideology, and Economics in Nazi Germany: The Reich Chambers of Music, Theater, and the Visual Arts.* Chapel Hill, NC: The University of North Carolina Press, 1993.

Sturani, Enrico. *Mussolini: Un dictateur en cartes postales.* Paris: Somogy Editions D'Art, 1997.

Tacchi, Francesca. *Storia illustrata del fascismo.* Florence, Italy: Giunti Editore, 2000.

Tannenbaum, Edward R. *The Fascist Experience, Italian Society and Culture, 1922–1945.* New York: Basic Books, 1972.

Taylor, Brandon. *Art and Literature Under the Bolsheviks.* London: Pluto Press, 1991.

Taylor, Brandon, and Wilfried van der Will, eds. *The Nazification of Art: Art, Design, Music, Architecture and Film in the Third Reich.* Winchester, England: The Winchester Press, 1990.

Topping, Seymour. *Journey Between Two Chinas.* New York: Harper and Row, 1974.

Trevor-Roper, H.R. *The Last Days of Hitler.* London: Macmillan Press, 1947.

Tucholsky, Mary, and Friedrich Lambert, eds. *Kurt Tucholsky und Deutschlands Marsch ins Dritte Reich.* Berlin: Verlag Alber Heinrich, 1938.

Tupitsyn, Margarita. *Gustav Klutsis and Valentina Kulagina: Photography and Montage After Constructivism.* Göttingen, Germany: Steidl, 2004.

Watson, Scott, and Shengtian Zheng. *Art of the Great Proletarian Cultural Revolution 1966–1976.* Vancouver: Morris and Helen Belkin Art Gallery, 2002.

Weapons of Mass Dissemination: the Propaganda of War. Miami: Wolfsonian–Florida International University, 2004.

White, Stephen. *The Bolshevik Poster.* New Haven, CT: Yale University Press, 1988.

Williams, Robert C. *Artists in Revolution: Portraits of the Russian Avant-garde, 1905–1925.* Bloomington, IN: Indiana University Press, 1977.

Willis, Harold Robert. *Sovietized Education: A Study of Soviet Education and Some of Its Effects.* New York: Exposition Press, 1965.

Yu, Frederick T.C. *Mass Persuasion in Communist China.* New York: Praeger, 1964.

Zeman, Z.A.B. *Nazi Propaganda.* London and New York: Oxford University Press, 1973.

Zhao, Zhong. *The Communist Program for Literature and Art in China.* Hong Kong: Union Research Institute, 1962.

Zhensheng, Li. *Red-Color News Soldier.* New York: Phaidon Press, 2003.

Zhisui, Li. *The Private Life of Chairman Mao: The Memoirs of Mao's Personal Physician.* New York: Random House, 1994.

index

illustration credits

Images are identified by picture numbers, except background images, which are identified by page number indicated by "p". Unless noted otherwise, all images are courtesy private collection.

© Austrian Archives/CORBIS: 14; © Bettmann/CORBIS: 17, 133, p1, p3, p22, p27, p32, p44 top, p71, p74, p79, p108, p127, p161, p170, p183, p193; Bundesarchiv: 90; © Henri Bureau/Sygma/CORBIS: p206; © CORBIS: 45, pp124–25; Courtesy Henry Drescher: 343–48, 396–405; Courtesy James Fraser: 233–44; © Marc Garanger/ CORBIS: p153; © Hulton-Deutsch Collection/CORBIS: 16, 132, p15, p31, p44 bottom, p47, p48, p62, p86, p99, p111, p116, p130, p205; Courtesy Mirko Ilic: 256–67; INTERFOTO/Friedrich: 6; ITAR-TASS: p165; Photo by Keystone Press: 349, 389, p4, pp172–73, p175, p184, p194, p197; The Kroul Collection at Hofstra University, Special Collections: 1, 82–85, 100–110, 113; © Ira Nowinski/CORBIS: p73; Scala/Art Resource, NY: 245; Snark/Art Resource, NY: 246; Courtesy Swann Gallery, New York: 247, 333; © Swim Ink 2, LLC/CORBIS: 3, 4; © Underwood & Underwood/CORBIS: 126; Courtesy of the United States Holocaust Memorial Museum Photo Archives: 121; Courtesy USM Books: 56; The Wolfsonian-Florida International University, Miami Beach, Florida. The Mitchell Wolfson, Jr. Collection: 41, 42, 46–48, 54–55, 62, 89, 91–92, 93–95, 115–16, 122–25, 129, 131, 141–42, 145–46, 149–50, 152, 164–65, 168–69, 171, 175–78, 198–202, 270–72; The Wolfsonian-Florida International University, Miami Beach, Florida. The Mitchell Wolfson, Jr. Collection Photo by Silvia Ros: 130, 137, 155, 231–32, 273–84; The Wolfsonian-Florida International University, Miami Beach, Florida. The Mitchell Wolfson, Jr. Collection Photo by Bruce White: 166; © Yevgeny Khaldei/CORBIS: p150, p162

acknowledgments

dedication

To my son, Nick Heller, may he always live in a democracy.

acknowledgements

This book would have been impossible without the instrumental support of my former editor Karen Stein at Phaidon Press in New York. Her good will and encouragement were essential in my achieving the completion of this project.

But if not for Valerie Vago-Laurer, my current editor, who shaped this manuscript, researched many of the documentary images, and acutely questioned me at every turn, I do not believe there would be a book at all. Thank you very much for your attention to detail and skillful editing.

Thanks also to my friends at Phaidon Press: managing editor Nancy Grubb for her enthusiasm, Karen Farquar and the production team for demanding the highest production standards, and art director Julia Hasting for her invaluable oversight. Also I cannot forget Vivian Constantinopoulos and Megan McFarland, former Phaidon editors, who helped in the very early stages.

The accessible design of this book was not easy to accomplish. Thanks to Adam Michaels of Project Projects, New York, for a brilliant job that wedded style and content.

Louise Fili, my wife, put up with my sleepless nights and other ravings while working on this book, and she helped translate the Italian section.

Much gratitude goes to the late Silas H. Rhodes and the Visual Arts Foundation, New York, for a research grant in the early stages of this project; David Rhodes, president of the School of Visual Arts for his emotional and monetary support; and Anthony Rhodes, executive vice president of the School of Visual Arts for his encouragement. Lita Talarico, co-chair of the MFA Design department, was always there for me during the more trying times of writing and research. And thanks to my former and current students at MFA Design, Lara McCormick, for her editorial assistance, and Clement Wu, Jia Chen, and Irina Lee (and her mom, Vera Nam) for helping with translations.

I am indebted, as always, to my brilliant researcher Jeff Roth, who provided me with the raw materials necessary to develop this narrative. Thanks also to photographers Adam Bell, who photographed my personal collection and the Hofstra collection, and Silvia Ros at the Wolfsonian Museum in Miami Beach.

My thanks to Cathy Leff, director of the Wolfsonian Museum at Florida International University in Miami, for bestowing upon me a fellowship to do research at her amazing repository of decorative and propaganda art. I am grateful in particular to the Mitchell Wolfson, Jr. Collection for making available many of the rare documents and artifacts used in this book. Thanks also to Frank Lucca, chief librarian, Marianne Lamonaca, curator, and Tim Hossler, art director of the Wolfsonian for their invaluable counsel while I was in Miami on the fellowship.

I greatly appreciate the generosity of the Kroul Collection at Hofstra University, Special Collections, for allowing me to use many of their prized rarities. And much gratitude to USM Books in Rapid City, South Dakota for providing me with access to their materials and information. Thank you all for your cooperation.

To the others who aided and abetted me in the research of these materials, I say thanks to Mirko Ilic, Jim Heimann, Victor Margolin, and David Lowenherz. Finally, thanks to my magazine editors who published early explorations of this material in their respective publications: Joyce Rutter Kaye and Martin Fox at *Print*, Hans Dieter Reichert at *Baseline*, and John L. Walters at *EYE*.

—Steven Heller

Phaidon Press Limited
Regent's Wharf
All Saints Street
London N1 9PA

Phaidon Press Inc.
180 Varick Street
New York, NY 10014

www.phaidon.com

First published 2008
© 2008 Phaidon Press Limited

ISBN 978 0 7148 4846 4

A CIP catalogue record for this book is available from the
British Library.

Designed by Project Projects, New York
Printed in Hong Kong

ISBN 978-0-7148-4846-4